PRAISE FOI

AND HIS BOOKS

"I am always looking for ideas that help people enrich their lives. This book does just that. I highly recommend you read it...it will feed your soul, lift your spirits, and help you live a fuller, richer, and more joy-filled life."

**—SARK (Susan Ariel Rainbow Kennedy),
author of *Living Juicy***

"Allen Klein is a noble and vital force watching over the human condition."

—Jerry Lewis, comedian

"I have come to know that sometimes the simplest words can make a major difference in how people perceive and interact with their world. This book can make that same difference to you."

—Jack Canfield, coauthor of *Chicken Soup for the Soul*

"Allen Klein's purpose is to make us feel inspired again, to bask in laughter and revel in joy."

—OMTimes

"A wonderful collection of timeless inspiration and powerful insights."

—Randy Gage, author of *Prosperity Mind*

"This book is guaranteed to inspire all who read it."

—Mike Robbins, author of *Focus on the Good Stuff*

"This book will wake you up and show you how this day may truly be the best day of your life."

—Kristine Carlson, coauthor of the *Don't Sweat the Small Stuff* series

"Allen's writing will lift your spirit and inspire you."

—Gloria Horsely, president and cofounder of Open to Hope

"Allen has packed enough fuel in this book to shine a light of positivity and hope that will glow for eternity."

—G. Brian Benson, author of *Habits for Success*

"Let Allen Klein inspire you and help you embrace and celebrate the joy in your life and in the life that surrounds you."

—Carole Brody Fleet, author of *Happily Even After*

"This fantastic book reminds us that while life can feel hectic and hurried, we need to slow down and rediscover the wonders of life. Combining research and heartwarming stories, Klein offers us an inspiring invitation to find the awe and wonder that surrounds us in our lives."

—Jonah Paquette, PsyD, author of *Awestruck, Real Happiness*, and *The Happiness Toolbox*

"Open the book and Open the Door to Awe and a whole lot of other good feelings. From butterflies to bees, music to mountains, we can find awe in anything and when we do, our

lives open up with wonder and joy. In his newest book, The Awe Factor, Allen Klein reminds us why it's essential that we cultivate and experience awe in our lives and just how we can do it. Open it up to any page, and you will feel delighted, calm, connected—and all that is awesome for sure."

—**Polly Campbell, author of** *How to Live an Awesome Life* **and** *Imperfect Spirituality*

"Every page of this wonder-full feast awakens life's essential glory. Trusty guide Allen Klein opens myriad gateways to awe—our natural birthright, and quite dearly needed today. Miraculous!"

—**Gary Gach, author of** *Pause, Breathe, Smile* **and** *The Complete Idiot's Guide to Buddhism*

"Reading Allen Klein's books is like spending special moments with a wise, funny, compassionate friend. This book will inspire readers to an ever-greater Life Appreciation."

—**Don Baird, PsyD, author of** *Suffering Is Highly Overrated*

"This must-read book will change the way you see your life and everything in it! Packed with incredible stories and actionable suggestions to recognize the AWE-filled moments in your life, you'll find this book inspirational, emotional, educational, and downright—dare I say it—awesome! Once you have this book you will never put it on your bookshelf again! You will dog-ear the pages, highlight the stories, and return again and again for the heart-filled feeding Allen Klein provides."

—**Rev. Dr. Cher Holton, Unity Minister at the Unity Center for YOUniversal Prosperity, Durham, NC**

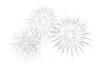

"If you think that awe is rarely experienced, I've got news for you. As The Awe Factor brilliantly reveals, true inspiration is available every moment of every day. This powerful book will help you be in awe of life with the promise of greater happiness and fulfillment."

—Marcia Wieder, CEO, Dream University and bestselling author

"Allen Klein's goal in this book is to help us have a richer and more enjoyable life. He succeeds beyond measure by bringing our attention to something that is almost indefinable... an experience of awe. A snapshot of an experience that we remember forever. An inexplicable moment that reminds us we are in the Presence of the Divine."

—Pragito Dove, author of *Lunchtime Enlightenment* and founder of DiscoverMeditation.com

"With so much focus on all that divides us, all the challenges we face and how difficult life is, there has never been a better time to view our current situation, our lives and our future through a radically different lens. Allen Klein reminds us not only that is it possible to still be in awe of the gifts of life, but provides clear steps so that we can live there."

—John O'Leary, bestselling author of *On Fire* and *In Awe*

"In The Awe Factor, Allen Klein captures the transcendent experience and power of awe, while also providing you countless examples from everyday life. It brought tears to my eyes and a smile to my lips. The perfect balance!"

—Rev. Ken Daigle, Senior Minister at Unity San Francisco

"This wonder-filled book will return you to the magic and power of that emotion we so often lose sight of—awe. Reading The Awe Factor *is good for your soul."*

—Dacher Keltner, professor of psychology, UC Berkeley

*"*The Awe Factor *is a powerful reminder of the wonder and mystery that is all around us. Allen Klein is inviting us all to open our awareness and see life with new eyes and a fresh perspective."*

—Rev. DeeAnn Weir Morency, Associate Minister at Unity San Francisco

"In this beautiful book, Allen Klein reminds us of the joy that is right inside when we get out of our head and connect with something much greater that both humbles and fills us with wonder. With anecdotes, pointers, wisdom, and delight The Awe Factor *helps us remember that in a moment we can shift our perspective and come alive. What a gift!"*

—James Baraz, coauthor of *Awakening Joy*

"As children, we were awe aficionados. Then we grow up and Adultitis dims our vision. Allen Klein is a master at helping us to see with new eyes and this book is a magic wand for bringing awe and wonder back into view."

—Jason Kotecki, artist and author of *A Chance of Awesome*

"In a world in which bad news seems much more prevalent than good, Allen Klein's book The Awe Factor *offers welcome and soul-healing relief. In a unique approach, Klein has examined every facet of awe's shining qualities so that the reader not only comes away with a deeper understanding and appreciation of*

awe's benefits, but also of life itself. It would be too easy to say that this book is awe-inspiring...but in fact it is; and it's not too much of a stretch to say that this little book will, as its subtitle suggests, make a big difference in your life!"

—Maggie Oman Shannon, author of *Prayers for Healing, Prayers for Hope and Comfort*, and *Crafting Calm*

"In *The Awe Factor, Allen Klein* reminds us that the experience of awe is available to all of us. You know the feeling; whether it's getting the chills when someone authentically shares their experience, when the words and music of a song resonate so deeply that we're certain it was written just for us, or the moon lights our path in the dark of night, awe captures our attention and fills our being with a sense of wonder. This is a perfect book for the time we're living when joy, wonder, and awe are needed nourishment for our soul. Thank you, Allen Klein, for creating this awesome book."

—Susyn Reeve, author of *Heart Healing* and creator of Wholehearted Living

"Allen Klein is one of those rare human beings who truly understands that life is more than what it seems, more than what we consciously know, and to live it fully we have to let invisible forces and things we can't understand do their magic. In this book, he inspires us to live in joy and wonder."

—David Friedman, composer and author of *We Can Be Kind*

"Plato told us philosophy begins in wonder. The Awe Factor will show you how and why and renew your sense of wonder."

—Sam Keen, author of *Apology for Wonder*

THE
AWE
FACTOR

OTHER WORKS BY ALLEN KLEIN:

The Joy of Simplicity

The Lighten Up Book

Positive Thoughts for Troubling Times

Embracing Life After Loss

You Can't Ruin My Day

Secrets Kids Know...That Adults Oughta Learn

Change Your Life! A Little Book of Big Ideas

Having the Time of Your Life

The Art of Living Joyfully

Always Look on the Bright Side

Words of Love

Mom's the Word

Inspiration for a Lifetime

The Courage to Laugh

The Healing Power of Humor

Learning to Laugh When You Feel Like Crying

L.A.U.G.H.: Using Humor and Play to Help Clients Cope

THE
AWE
FACTOR

How a Little Bit of Wonder Can Make a Big Difference in Your Life

ALLEN KLEIN

Bestselling author of
The Healing Power of Humor

Conari
Press

CORAL GABLES

Cover Design and Interior Layout Design: Jermaine Lau

Published by Conari Press, an imprint of Mango Publishing, a division of Mango Media Inc.

For permission requests, please contact the publisher at:

Mango Publishing Group
2850 Douglas Road, 2nd Floor
Coral Gables, FL 33134 USA
info@mango.bz

For special orders, quantity sales, course adoptions and corporate sales, please email the publisher at sales@mango.bz. For trade and wholesale sales, please contact Ingram Publisher Services at customer.service@ingramcontent.com or +1.800.509.4887.

The Awe Factor: How a Little Bit of Wonder Can Make a Big Difference in Your Life

ISBN: (p) 978-1-64250-403-3 (e) 978-1-64250-404-0

BISAC: SEL016000, SELF-HELP / Personal Growth / Happiness

LCCN:

To everyone who shared their awe moment with me for this book and for those who have ever brought a bit of awe into my life, thank you.

For that, I am most grateful.

*Our goal should be to live life in radical amazement...
get up in the morning and look at the world in a way that
takes nothing for granted. Everything is phenomenal;
everything is incredible; never treat life casually.*

—Rabbi Abraham Joshua Heschel

TABLE OF CONTENTS

PART THREE
AWE-WAKENING PRESCRIPTIONS

FOREWORD

In a recent post on Twitter, I wrote, "There are always ways we can improve, both big and small." That is why I love *The Awe Factor*. This landmark book will help you discover the everyday magical moments in your life in order to improve it.

Klein shows readers that we don't have to take a trip to the Grand Canyon or see a double rainbow to be awestruck. As the heartfelt stories in the book illustrate, opportunities for awe abound...if we are open to them.

Awe is the new happiness. Although not studied much in the past, this important emotion has recently captured the attention of researchers and scientists. Recent studies have shown that awe can help us connect to others, lower our stress levels, and increase our compassion, among other benefits. In other words, it can help us be both healthier and happier.

With a sprinkling of the spiritual, the scientific, and the everyday, *The Awe Factor* echoes a lot of what I've taught and believed for years. And it does so from a new and refreshing angle—how seeing the world through the eyes of awe can enrich our lives.

Perhaps my favorite parts of the book are the firsthand awe-related stories. Like those in my Chicken Soup books, these stories not only amaze and enchant but may even bring a tear or two to your eyes.

The Awe Factor is the perfect book for our challenging times. Not only because of its inspiring stories but also because of two other attributes. It will make you aware of awe's numerous life-changing benefits, and it will show you how easy it is to get more awe in your life.

All of the books I've written have a common theme. They are all geared toward inspiring readers to improve their life. That's why I am so fond of Allen Klein's latest book. It too will make readers' lives better.

Klein's first book, *The Healing Power of Humor*, was a groundbreaker and a classic in the therapeutic humor field. This book, *The Awe Factor*, is also a trailblazer. Read it and you will discover a whole new world. Get your copy now. It's awesome!

Jack Canfield, coauthor of the

Chicken Soup for the Soul series

Santa Barbara, California

PART ONE

ASPECTS OF AWE

He stared out at the ocean and said, "Look at the view, young lady. Look at the view." And every day, in some little way, I try to do what he said. I try to look at the view. That's all. Words of wisdom from a man with not a dime in his pocket, no place to go, nowhere to be. Look at the view. When I do what he said, I am never disappointed.

—Anna Quindlen,
A Short Guide to a Happy Life

In the Broadway play *The Search for Signs of Intelligent Life in the Universe,* based on Jane Wagner's book of the same name, Lily Tomlin plays the character of Trudy the bag lady. At one point in the play, she is awed by a night sky filled with stars and declares that each day, henceforth, she is going to do "awe-robics."

If I had to choose one word to describe this book, it would be Trudy the bag lady's made-up word—*awe-robics.* I say that because *The Awe Factor* will help you strengthen your awe muscles.

Like having a personal trainer, this book will broaden your view of awe with inspiring examples of awe moments from my own and other people's lives. Like regular exercise, it will also discuss the benefits you can derive from it. And finally, like a gym schedule, it will give you suggestions for how to incorporate awe exercises into your daily routine.

So, put on your gym clothes and let's begin.

WHAT IS AWE?

What it is that dwelleth here
I know not
Yet my heart is full of awe
and the tears trickle down.

—Eleventh century Japanese poem

DEFINING/DESCRIBING AWE

After showing my former literary agent my idea for *The Awe Factor*, he asked me to define "awe." I was hard pressed to come up with an encompassing definition. Depending which dictionary you use, it can be "an emotion variously combining dread, veneration, and wonder that is inspired by authority or by the sacred or sublime," or a little more to my liking, "an overwhelming feeling of reverence, admiration, fear, etc., produced by that which is grand, sublime, extremely powerful, or the like."

In a nutshell, the most common definition of awe involves the notion that it contains the elements of both fear and wonder. Think, for example, of a thunderstorm. It, along with the accompanying lightning, frequently creates both wonder and fear at the same time. Who, as a child, has not hidden under a blanket during a thunderstorm and peeked out to see the magnificence of the lightning?

And yet, not all awe experiences contain fear—especially more common ones, like beholding a newborn or being awestruck by a child's laughter.

Just as it is hard to define awe, so too is it often difficult to describe the experience. Some people associate awe with such things as synchronicity, coincidence, or perhaps a higher power. Others might use words like enchanted, blissful, bedazzled, mystical, mesmerized, or even ecstatic to convey how they felt during their awe event.

In addition, certain phrases pop up on a regular basis when people attempt to describe their awe moment. One of them is "it gave me goose bumps."

Awe Fact

The number one cause of goose bumps is a change of temperature. The second greatest cause of goose bumps is awe.

Other phrases people frequently use to talk about their awe experience are:

- "boggled my mind"
- "floored me"
- "left me speechless"
- "took my breath away"
- "made my hair stand on end"

(I probably would never utter the last one, because I'm nearly bald.)

Professionals Define Awe

Dacher Keltner and Jonathan Haidt, psychologists:

A sense of wonder and amazement that occurs when one is inspired by great knowledge, beauty, sublimity, or might. It's the experience of confronting something greater than yourself. Awe expands one's frame of reference and drives self-transcendence. It encompasses admiration and inspiration and can be evoked by everything from great works of art or music to religious transformation, from breathtaking natural landscapes to human feats of daring and discovery... Awe is a complex emotion and frequently involves a sense of surprise, unexpectedness, or mystery.

Jonah Paquette, psychologist:

The feeling we get in the presence of something vast that challenges our understanding of the world.

Paul Pearsall, neuropsychologist:

Awe is a sacred hunch, an overwhelming emotion that indicates that something within us is sensing something about the world that our brain has yet to discover.

David Delgado, visual strategist at NASA's Jet Propulsion Lab:

It feels like magic, amazement, mystery, reverence. It's the moment when we realize it's a gift and privilege to be alive.

Alan Morinis, anthropologist:

Awe arises when we encounter life and the world in ways that breach the ordinary.

Hopefully, after reading about the various aspects of awe, you will come to your own conclusion about how to define and describe it. Hopefully too, you will realize why you need to get regular "awe-robics" in your life.

ATTRIBUTES OF AWE

Awe is there to be had in any moment. When you walk outside, stop to look at the garden, watch or even hear children playing, observe an act of kindness, or feel an intimacy... To open ourselves to these moments without reservations...makes it possible to gain more of the gift these moments hold for us.

—Alan Morinis, *Everyday Holiness*

Magnificent and Humbling

To be in awe for me seems to encompass both our magnificence and our humility all at the same time. We are insignificant specks on the one hand. And yet we are a part of a universe that is beautiful and bold beyond our imagination.

—Nancy LeTourneau, *Horizons*

To me, awe is a combination of two things basically. Firstly, we see the magnificence of the thing we are seeing, its glorious majesty. We are blown away by the vastness, the scale, the seeming impossibility of its existence, yet here it is. It makes us feel our smallness, makes us feel humble, and that is a wonderful thing.

Secondly...for me awe contains another important element. As well as feeling humble, witnessing the magnificence of the "other" connects us to everything. It makes us feel at one. And this allows us to also feel our own magnificence! So we feel the combination of humility and magnificence at the same time. And that is truly incredible.

—Cathy Broome, on Quora.com

Grand and Amazing

Awe often comes in the presence of something grand and amazing. It challenges our worldview and makes us feel small in the presence of something bigger than ourselves.

—James Jay, on Quora.com

Awe is unexplained wonder, when you see the power of creation in unexpected places. When a power bigger than me has presented itself.

—Mary Yonekawa

Connecting and Comforting

Awe is an overwhelming and bewildering sense of connection with a starling universe that is usually far beyond the narrow band of our consciousness.

—Paul Pearsall, *AWE*

Every time I go outside at night, I look up. I stare at the moon, trace the constellations, search for planets. There's something remarkably humbling and awe-inspiring about it. These lights have been hanging above our heads since before anything resembling humans existed. Their light traveled for millions of years to reach our eyes. What we're seeing is a glimpse of the past. It's a reminder that in the grand scheme of things, we're as tiny and fleeting as the photons shooting through space. The universe was here long before us, and it will be here long after us. I find that to be a strangely comforting thought.

—Jessica Taylor, on Quora.com

Transcending and Unexplainable

To me awe-inspiring experiences transcend us out of our everyday lives. We are in the present moment, fully. Sometimes we may have an out-of-body experience. In this moment I felt that my body dissolved into nature around me. There was no separation. I felt at one with the Divine source.

—Maureen Calamia, author of *Creating Luminous Spaces*

For me, awe is something not understandable but uplifts me to a more divine concept of the event. Maybe I don't understand what is going on, but I have a feeling that there is a certain divine operation in process. You know, here's the deal—I don't know what awe is. That is part of it. Not being able to explain an event in human terms.

—Noreen Halvey

If you think of feelings you have when you are awed by something—for example, knowing that elements in your body trace to exploded stars—I call that a spiritual reaction, speaking of awe and majesty, where words fail you.

—Neil deGrasse Tyson, astrophysicist

Moving and Insightful

A moment of being emotionally struck by something or having a moment of insight or revelation.

—Steve Sultanoff, psychologist

There is a feeling of wonder within you, you cease becoming the center of your own universe. The thing you are viewing could be a very usual thing: a tree, a bird, the teeming humanity in a city. Yet you are perceiving it all on a higher, deeper, and more intimate level.

—Tristan Marajh, on Quora.com

Overpowering

Awe is that moment when you see something which creates such a beating in your heart and soul that everything else seems to disappear or become unimportant. It's that moment when everything seems to stop. To me it's the embodiment of the saying, "took my breath away."

—Bron Roberts

Fleeting, yet Ever-Present

[Awe is] a feeling in my chest that literally makes my mouth involuntarily open and often brings tears to my eyes... Something that will never happen again—and something you remember forever.

—Robyn Vie Carpenter-Brisco, spiritual life coach and author

NATURE-MADE AWE

Most people can tell you about a time when they were soothed, inspired, or awed while contemplating the natural world. The settings may vary but the feelings are universal.

—Frederic and Mary Ann Brussat, *Spiritual Literacy*

I used to own a house in the country about an hour-and-a-half drive north of San Francisco. It was a little over an acre of property. It had no view of the nearby ocean, but I used to kid about its "partial ocean view," since, on some days, if you walked down the road a bit, you could see a sliver of ocean shimmering in the sun.

What it did provide was not only something I could meditate upon for hours but also a chance to witness the awe of nature if I sat still enough to observe it. The open flat field seemed pretty much uneventful. A leaf perhaps blew a few feet across the grassy surface once in a while or a bird or a butterfly flew by from time to time. It was only if I sat there long enough and looked closer that I was awed by the enormity of the activity happening right before my eyes—a snail making its way up a tree trunk, a yellow canary plucking a berry from the nearby pyracanth shrub, a spider weaving an intricate web between the bars of the porch railing.

The classic example of an awe-inducing natural phenomenon is, of course, the Grand Canyon. But there are other, less grandiose occurrences in nature that can also provide those awe moments. I remember one when I was growing up in a fifth-floor walk-up apartment in the Bronx. My world was filled with concrete and brick. Every summer I'd plant lima beans in a small wooden cheese box on the fire escape. I'd watch the vines twist around the metal railings and get bigger and bigger. I never got any lima beans, but the green leaves were enough to amaze me.

Looking back, I think I was in awe at how one small, seemingly dried-up hard bean could produce so much life. I'm still amazed every time I plant an almost dead-looking gladiola bulb in my garden and see it produce a tall, magnificent, beautifully colored flower, or when I see how the tiniest of seeds can turn into such a dazzling orange poppy.

Sunrise and Sunsets

AWE FACTOR: BEYOND BELIEF

This morning, someone posted an untouched photo on Facebook of the sunrise from their apartment in San Francisco. The bottom of the photo was yellow, then as you went up the sunrise, the colors changed to pink, orange, burned sienna, brown, and finally black near the top. The person posting labeled it, "Beyond Belief"—and it was. I could only imagine how much more brilliant the actual sunrise was. I also thought about how difficult it is to describe an awesome sunrise or a sunset to someone else. Or the green flash that sometimes happens during a Hawaiian sunset? As in many awe experiences, you have to be there to believe it.

The Stars

AWE FACTOR: OVERWHELMING

It has been calculated by scientists that there are ten times more stars in the night sky than grains of sand in the world's deserts and beaches. Is it any wonder then that we are awed by them?

I distinctly remember, after a long night talking with a friend, sitting in my car and looking up at the stars, just admiring their beauty. And it suddenly struck me how small the earth is, and, by extension, I am, in all of that vastness. And "struck" is the right word, as it was sudden realization. It wasn't that I hadn't understood that intellectually before, but it hit me much more viscerally in that moment. And it was both a frightening and a soothing thought, at the same time.

—James Martin, on Quora.com

[I experienced awe] the first time I ventured West and stood at a high altitude, far from any city, so that there was no light anywhere to interrupt the brilliant display of stars in the night sky. You could see the clusters, the bands, the planets, and when I awoke from a few hours of sleep in the travel van... I stumbled outside and just froze in place. It's rare that I truly gasp in awe, but I did, and I felt an emotional flood that made the

hairs on my arms stand up. I'd never seen anything like it before.

—Mark Hughes, Quora.com

My favorite position for viewing the stars is lying on my back looking up from the earth. It lets me contemplatively take in this spacious nighttime majesty. Surrounded by mountains and trees, this evening's view of the big sky is somewhat limited, but I can still see a sizable opening of sky above... Silently I let the heavens cover me with darkness and mystery and what I call my soul-to-sky connection. The twin sisters of solitude and silence are seductively present in this dark landscape. Wordlessly they lead me into their heavenly chambers, and I am wrapped in their charmed presence. Enveloped in the dark, I sense that I am in the presence of something sacred.

—Richard Broderick, *Leather Tramp Journal*

Grand Canyon

I've been blessed with many moments of awe in my life. One I remember distinctly was when I was eleven and a half or twelve. My parents, my two brothers, and I were on a cross-country driving trip. We were headed to the Grand Canyon. As we approached the canyon, there are a couple of places along the road where you can pull off to see this incredible vista.

My father stopped the car and we just sort of fell out, struck by the overwhelming sense of vast spaciousness. Even my older teenage brother just shut up being blown away by the sight. The awe, the sense of depth, the size, the grandness was quite amazing.

That was the main level of awe. But it was not that or the looks of my family's faces. It was all the other people. They all were just blown away by this sense of God, actually, of awe, of oneness. It was like that which separated people just melted away because our defenses were melted away. We were just in that moment.

And it was a moment I will never forget.

—Dave Cooperberg

Trees

AWE FACTOR: TIMELESS

I remember hearing a lecture by Dewitt Jones who was a photojournalist for *National Geographic* magazine at the time. I was astounded not only by his stories but by his jaw-dropping photographs and how he captured them. I remember one in particular in which he was with a group of other photographers documenting the massive California redwood trees. Jones showed the audience some of the incredible shots he had taken that day.

Then he went on to tell us how he stayed behind after the other professional photographers left. He felt that, in spite of the great photos he took that day, there was still one more that would top them all. And he was right.

At just the right moment, he lay down on the ground under a giant redwood tree, looked up, and captured hundreds of rainbow prisms of the sun radiating out from behind the redwood branches.

When he showed this slide, there was an audible gasp that spontaneously erupted from the audience. The photo was something that couldn't be described or understood with words. And perhaps that is what awe is...something that can't be put into words, but which is moving and connects people through a common experience.

Oceans

AWE FACTOR: VAST

One day I was driving on Highway 1 that parallels the Pacific Ocean on the California coast. The road suddenly climbed up a hill and took me above the dense fog. I looked down and felt like I was in heaven. Nothing but puffy layers of white rolling fog below me and crystal-clear blue sky above. That moment, when the road broke through the fog and descended toward a vast shimmering ocean, as far as my eyes could see, with its white-capped waves, was awe-inspiring. It indeed took my breath away.

A few times when I was a kid, my aunt would take us to Old Orchard Beach in Maine. I remember the first time I saw the sea, I stopped dead in my tracks absolutely mesmerized, mouth hanging open in wonder.

I don't know how long I stood there, but my brother came along and whacked me on the head telling me to stop staring and get the suitcase from the car. I was startled back into the real world and I still remember that feeling of wanting to stay lost in the magic of the ocean...

That first trip to the beach changed my life forever.

As an adult, I joined the Navy and spent lots of time on the water and on beaches around the world. I have never lost my sense of wonder and awe and I treasure each journey I get to make to the ocean.

—Michael Shook, on Quora.com

For me it's a local beach. It's hidden behind a hill, so you have to trudge up the hill, all you can see is the sky and the hill and then you reach the crest and suddenly the beach and ocean appear. There is beach in either direction as far as you can see, and the ocean disappears into the horizon. I will never grow tired of the awe that view inspires.

—Bron Roberts

Diana Nyad is a long-distance swimmer who was the first person to swim from Cuba to Florida. It was her fifth attempt and she did it without the aid of a shark cage. It was more than a hundred miles of traveling on a treacherous ocean.

In one of her TED talks, she says swimming for fifty-three hours "was an intense and unforgettable life experience." In speaking about the wonder of it all, she reveals that she is not a religious person "but I'll tell you...to be in the azure blue of the Gulf Stream...looking down miles and miles and miles...to feel the majesty of this blue planet we live on, it's awe-inspiring."

My very favorite thing to do this time of year—both to honor the New Year and in honor of my birthday...is to go to the ocean. There's something heart-opening, to me, about seeing the expanse of the sea before you, particularly on a cold sunny day... The world feels big and everything feels possible. All your petty worries fall away, and even the not-petty serious problems can start to feel surmountable. It's one of the most freeing and empowering practices I know, and in the spirit of start-as-you-mean-to-go-on, I can think of no better energy with which to imbue the twelve months ahead.

**—Bridget Watson Payne,
editorial director at Chronicle Books**

Rain and Clouds

AWE FACTOR: AMAZING

In *The Book of Awesome,* author Neil Pasricha writes about his fondness for rain: "There is just something about the smell of rain on a hot sidewalk. It's sort of like the rain cleans the air—completely hammering all the dirt and grime particles down to the ground and releasing some hot, baked-in chemicals from the pavement. It smells best if it hasn't rained in a while and the sidewalk is scalding hot. That is sort of sizzles and steams up into a big, hot, intoxicating whiff. Awesome!"

And in his book *The Sacred Journey,* Frederick Buechner writes about his experience of rain when he was a youngster:

> I loved the rain as a child. I loved the sound of it on the leaves of trees and roofs and windowpanes and umbrellas and the feel of it on my face and bare legs. I love the hiss of rubber tires on rainy streets and the flip-flop of windshield wipers. I loved the smell of wet grass and raincoats and the shaggy coats of dogs. A rainy day was a special day for me in a sense that no other kind of day was—a day when the ordinariness of things was suspended with ragged skies drifting to the color of pearl and dark streets turning to dark rivers of reflected light and even people transformed somehow as the rain drew them closer by giving them something to think about together, to take common shelter from, to complain of and joke about in ways that made them more like friends than it seemed to me they were on ordinary sunny days.

One Cloud

Try designing a system capable of suspending a billion pounds of water in midair with no strings attached.

It's called a cloud... How amazing it is that even a modest-size cloud, an "everyday" cloud like a cumulus a half mile high and wide, weighs...almost 1.5 billion pounds... A good-size cumulonimbus cloud, a thunderhead five or six miles on either side...weighs nearly fourteen billion pounds. One cloud.

—Gregg Levoy, *Vital Signs*

My Mom took her first flight when she was eighty-two. For years I tried to get her to fly, but nothing I did or said would get her off the ground. Then one day she won a round-trip airline ticket. So, finally she got on a plane.

I met her at the airport as she deplaned and anxiously asked her how she enjoyed the trip. Even though she was far from being a youngster, she experienced something that was not unlike the awesome moment I had watching my cousin take off in a plane when I was younger.

She proclaimed, "Oh, it was wonderful. I got to see the tops of the clouds!"

Hurricanes and Thunderstorms

AWE FACTOR: FEARSOME AND WONDERFUL

My friend and spiritual teacher John Welshons shared a story with me about his confrontation of a hurricane.

"I'm thinking back on my childhood, the first experience of awe that I recall was being in Atlantic City, New Jersey, during the summer when Hurricane Donna arrived." Welshons remembers,

> We were in an apartment right on the boardwalk, essentially right on the beach. I was about ten or eleven years old and staying there with my mother and sister. We didn't have the good sense to leave and by the time we figured out that we should evacuate, it was too late.

> So, we stayed on the third floor of this beachfront apartment overlooking the ocean. The sandy beach, which was probably a hundred yards from the water's edge to the boardwalk, all disappeared at the height of the storm. Waves were breaking over the boardwalk, while parts of it were breaking away. The ocean now coming into the street.

Looking back, Welshons says,

> I probably should have felt frightened, but I didn't. I just felt awestruck. It was just this sense of something that was so much more powerful than us. And I couldn't perceive that it had any ill intent. It was just a storm doing its thing...a storm being a storm. It cultivated this strange sense of peace in me, in spite of the fact that

the wind was howling and the ocean was swallowing up the land.

One of the interesting things about Welshons's story is that, in spite of it having the potential for illustrating the classic definition of awe consisting of both wonder and fear, he was awed but instead of fear he found peace.

Thunder

There is something about the energy of a storm that makes me feel good. I love the smell of a storm, that warm dramatic side lighting before it hits. Most of all, I love the rumble and crash of thunder.

—Joy Crotty, on Quora.com

Snow and Snowflakes

AWE FACTOR: WONDERFUL

I no longer live on the East Coast so my encounters with snow have been more limited than they used to be. But thinking about snow brought back memories of when I lived on the corner of Third Avenue and 31st Street in New York City. The noise level of the passing cars, trucks barreling down Third Avenue, or the blare of fire engines and ambulances was deafening. Then, when it snowed, all would be still. And if it snowed during the night, even before I looked out the window, I knew the city would be blanketed with white because it was so quiet.

When I think about snow, I also think about the marvel that it is. As each snowflake falls through the clouds, the different temperatures and moisture levels change each one. It used to be believed that every single snowflake was different from every other. More recent investigation has revealed that there are only thirty-five different shapes. All unique, however, in that they are each molecularly different. And the only way to see that is to look closer. Real close. Under a microscope, in fact.

On the second season of the Netflix series *Abstract,* Israeli-born designer Neri Oxman talks about her first encounter with snow, "I remember as a kid growing up, waking up in the middle of a storm night." She opened the window of her bedroom terrace to discover something she had never seen before:

> It all felt so incredibly magical. I remember grabbing a piece of that substance, putting it in a plastic bag, and putting it under my pillow, waiting to show my parents this magical material that fell from the sky. I remember waking up with this wet bed and being so extremely disappointed, trying to make sense of it all.

Oxman concludes, "I think that sense of awe and wonder that I had as a three-year-old, who never saw snow, stayed with me. And that innocence is still there. I hope it is still there."

Perfection

Have you ever seen anything more perfect than a snowflake? Its intricacy, its design, its symmetry, its conformity to itself and originality from all else—all are a mystery. You wonder at the miracle of this awesome display of Nature.

—Neale Donald Walsch, *Conversations with God*

While sitting at my desk today, I looked up and out the window to see gigantic snowflakes floating swiftly from the sky. There were so many flakes that it appeared to be white confetti falling. This experience inspired awe in me because it was beautiful, yet in the same moment, it was also terrifying to think about having to drive in it. I decided to release the fear of driving in it and relish in the moment by just watching the snow fall. I imagined the silence that accompanies a snowstorm—it was inspiring.

—Lisa McGrath, on Quora.com

Butterflies

AWE FACTOR: ASTONISHING

A book could easily be written about the thousands upon thousands of different species of animals, birds, and insects and all of their awesome qualities. For example, did you know that an elephant is the only animal that cannot jump? That the kangaroo can jump headfirst into their mother's pouch? That giraffes give birth standing up?

One of the creatures of the world that often gets an automatic awe response is the butterfly. Even without knowing about their miraculous transition—one day they are a caterpillar crawling on the ground and the next they are flying above it—the butterfly is truly remarkable. I've been awed by them for years.

One summer I rented a house on Fire Island, which is a long barrier island off the shore of Long Island, New York. I was walking on one of the narrow boardwalks that connects the bay and the ocean. I suddenly saw this tree with beautiful rustling orange leaves. Except it wasn't leaves. As I got closer, I noticed that they were monarch butterflies. Thousands of them huddled together clinging to the tree branches.

Years later I found out that every fall, millions of monarchs fly from southern Canada and the northern and central part of the United States to hibernate in Mexico. In the spring, they mate and return north again. Sometimes these seemingly fragile insects travel as much as two thousand miles on their journey.

What is even more wondrous is that the monarchs generally arrive just before the Mexican celebration of the Day of the Dead, a time of prayer, remembrance, and celebration of friends and family members who have died. It is believed that the monarchs are the spirits of loved ones returning on the wings of the butterflies.

No one really knows why the monarchs are the only insects that make such a long and risky journey. But the mystery surrounding their migration, the beauty of seeing so many of them in flight, the way they huddle together in the trees, and the added Mexican folklore certainly make for a truly astounding and awesome phenomenon.

Honeybees

AWE FACTOR: INSPIRING

For Kathy Laurenhue, owner of Wiser Now, Inc. and author of *Creating Delight: Connecting Gratitude, Humor, and Play for All Ages*, awe is "easily discovered if you are looking for it."

Laurenhue notes:

> Nature is my go-to source for awe when it is late in the day and I need to squeeze in soul-satisfying exercise. If I have to choose just one example from Mother Nature, let's make it honeybees. I could easily list the mind-boggling facts about honeybees National Geographic style. Instead, here's my version of why they fill me with awe:

- A honeybee hive is a highly successful matriarchal society that performs a vital role for our planet through pollination.
- The queen works as hard as her subjects, laying 600 to 2,500 eggs *every* day.
- These female bees communicate and cooperate by joyful dancing, showing each other the way to the nectar sources.
- They find these nectar sources through their remarkable eyesight which includes ultraviolet light, so they are always drawn to beauty.
- When they are tired, they nap—in flowers no less.

Awww, what could be cuter?

"Yep," concludes Laurenhue, "if I had to be an insect, and couldn't be a caterpillar (Eat a lot. Sleep for a while. Wake up beautiful.) I'd opt for being an awesome honeybee."

The Cosmos

AWE FACTOR: OVERWHELMING

If you are still uncertain about awe in the world, consider the following three things:

- 118 different kinds of atoms make up everything in the universe.
- Those atoms come together in a way which allow us, and all beings, to be alive.
- Earth is traveling through the universe at the rate of 483,000 miles an hour...and you can still sit and read this book without falling off your chair.

Childbirth

AWE FACTOR: MIRACULOUS

Next to nature, childbirth is the second most mentioned phenomenon described as producing awe. In spite of the fact that there are 360,000 babies born every day in the world, this common occurrence can still produce reactions of wonder both in those directly involved in the birthing as well as in those who simply find themselves around babies.

A number of people I interviewed commented that this was one of their most memorable awe-related experiences in their life.

"Giving birth, then when the baby is placed on my chest and breast fed...wow!"

"When I looked at my baby for the first time, [and I] saw those beautiful eyes."

"I am awestruck over and over by babies. That open look, and their laugh."

I totally agree. I remember when my daughter was born. It was just past midnight when I saw the nurse scurry down the hall with a bassinet. I ran after her thinking my newborn was in it. She laughed when I caught up with her and informed me that the bassinet was empty; she hadn't picked my daughter up yet, she was on the way to get her. And then there she was. This perfect little being. Such tiny hands with such tiny fingers. All perfect and all awesome.

> When my daughter was born, crying and a weird purple color, the nurses brought her to me. I looked at her and said, "Hi, my baby Emma. I'm your dad and I will love you forever." The moment I spoke to her she stopped crying instantly! I had to fight the tears from pouring out of me! It was and is the greatest gift I will ever receive... Nothing can make you feel pain and love like a child can. That was my awe moment.
>
> —Joshua Smith, on Quora.com

I think my brain broke when I first saw my daughter. I looked down at her and I honestly was not able to process what I was seeing. It was almost like my brain shorted out and was being rewired as I looked at her. The experience was almost religious in how it felt.

—Robert Devaux, on Quora.com

Giving birth. Looking down at that little boy and thinking, "I would die for you." And subsequently discovering parts of my heart that I had not known existed.

—Marlene Dempster, on Quora.com

True Miracle

Obviously, there is pain in childbirth. But giving birth is also a moment of awe and wonder, a moment when the true miracle of aliveness, and of a woman's amazing part in that miracle, is suddenly experienced in every cell of one's body. It is in that sense truly an altered state of consciousness.

—Riane Eisler, *Sacred Pleasure*

HUMAN-MADE AWE

The truth is, we are surrounded by so many wonders that we are spoiled by them. We are witnesses to miracles, all of us, every single day. Wondrous acts of creativity so marvelous that if we actually looked at them with new eyes, we'd be left awestruck.

—Jason Kotecki, author of *A Chance of Awesome*

Theater

AWE FACTOR: CAPTIVATING

I just returned from a week in New York City. Now that I live in San Francisco I travel there at least once a year to see friends and family, but mostly to see Broadway shows. I was born and raised in the city and was awed when I saw my first Broadway show at seven years old. Later, in high school, I would take the subway downtown to see a matinee every Saturday. It was the inspiration for my becoming a scenic designer for theater and television.

I know that movies create spectacular effects that could never be duplicated on stage, but there is something magical about seeing live actors perform.

It wasn't until now, writing about awe, that I realized the connection between my being awed by what I saw and a spiritual experience. After all, the performers were sharing their God-given talent. The performance was an expression and a link to some higher power.

The same is true of magnificent moments of stagecraft. They too are a result of God-given talent and thus connected to a higher source.

I can give many examples of stagecraft that have awed me. But the one that stands out was the simplest, and perhaps that is why it was so powerful. It is the last scene in the musical *Fiddler on the Roof*. The people of the town of Anatevka are forced to leave the village where they have lived for generations. Leaving most of their possessions behind, they start walking away, many of them not knowing where they will end up.

What little scenery there was is taken away, leaving a bare and barren stage with nothing but a turntable. The immigrants, burdened with their belongings, move ever so slowly on the turntable, singing bittersweetly about Anatevka, leaving behind the town they loved so much.

Truly it is an awe-moving moment.

Cirque du Soleil

AWE FACTOR: BREATHTAKING

"They say there are five senses... We've trapped a sixth..." notes the Cirque du Soleil website. "Take off into the extraordinary. Feel unstoppable goose bumps. Live indescribable moments. Catch a rare thrill. All that you feel is pure, incredible, AWE."

And this is no sales-pitch hyperbole. I've been to many Cirque shows and inevitably I am awestruck over and over again. Their shows encompass the true meaning of the word *awe*—both fear and wonder at the same time.

In the show *O*, for example, performers dive from the top rafters of the theater into a water-filled stage one moment, and in the next, performers are walking on the water. Or in *Kà*, in which a sand-filled stage tilts upright allowing the sand to cascade into the pit. Meanwhile performers slide down the vertical plain and stop by grabbing onto a peg that suddenly juts out to rescue them.

Perhaps the Cirque du Soleil moment that captured the truest meaning of awe for me was not anything mechanical or related to stagecraft. It was about a person in their steampunk-themed show *Kurios*. One performer, Antanina Satsura, makes her entrance by popping out of the belly of another performer. I first thought she was some sort of perfectly formed mechanized doll. But my heart sank when I realized that this was no doll. It was an extremely small human being—one of the ten smallest people in the world. She was perfectly proportioned and measured only three feet and two inches tall and weighed a mere forty pounds. Throughout the show, I was mesmerized; I could not take my eyes off her. She truly inspired my sense of awe.

Cirque Research

Neuroscientist Beau Lotto used Cirque to validate the importance of awe. He and his team recorded the brain activity of people before watching performances of *O*, as well as during the show.

They found, among other things, that awe can enhance our willingness to explore the unknown, including by making us more empathetic toward others.

In his TED talk, Lotto gives an example of how this might apply to conflict. "What if awe could enable us to enter conflict in at least two different ways? One, to give us the humility and courage to *not* know—to enter conflict with a question instead of an answer—to enter conflict with uncertainty instead of certainty? And second, in entering conflict that way, to seek to understand, rather than to convince."

While exploring people's reactions to Cirque du Soleil's performances, Lotto's team found a number of other benefits of awe. They include, among others:

- enhanced willingness to explore the unknown
- increased empathy toward others
- raised risk tolerance
- decreased the effect of stress
- increased creativity

I can measure my life by the moments when art transformed me—standing in front of Michelangelo's *Duomo Pieta*, listening to Dylan Thomas read his poetry, hearing Bach's cello suites for the first time.

But not only there...

It can happen anywhere, anytime. You do not have to be in some setting hallowed by greatness, or in the presence of an artist honored around the world. Art can work its magic any time...

Once you love an art enough that you can be taken up in it, you are able to experience an echo of the great creative act that mysteriously has given life to us all.

It may be the closest any of us can get to God.

—Kent Nerburn, *Letters to My Son*

Music

AWE FACTOR: TRANSCENDENT

In spite of the fact that I've designed a number of operas when I was a scenic designer, I'm not a big opera fan. My love is musical theater. However, every once in a while, I hear an aria from an opera that blows me away. I don't know their names, but there are several in *La Bohème* and *Madama Butterfly* that fit that bill.

Other music can be transformative too. Great symphonies, powerful rock concerts, and Gregorian chants, can, among others, awe us too.

Art

AWE FACTOR: MESMERIZING

Like a moment in the theater, a piece of artwork can also be so powerful, so amazing, that it can bring visceral excitement or create a reverence or calmness. I recall feeling the latter not too long ago at the Museum of Modern Art in San Francisco. It happened while viewing an installation by French artist Céleste Boursier-Mougenot. It was a simple concept but one with a profound effect.

The installation *clinamen v.3* was set in a room with a large round pool in the center of it and built-in benches surrounding. The expansive, intense blue water had dozens of white porcelain bowls floating in it. Swept along by the currents and heated water, the floating bowls gently came in contact with each other creating a soothing soundscape.

The piece mesmerized me. Later, when I analyzed why, I realized it touched me on several levels. The visual—the pure-white bowls randomly interacted with each other, not unlike the way humans move among other beings. The audio—like the sound of Tibetan bowls that resonate deep within us, never duplicating any sound a second time, thus keeping everything fresh and new. Then too, there was the gently calming movement of the water and, like some awe-related experiences, a certain fear that at any time the bowls might collide with each other too violently and break.

I had forgotten how powerful a piece of art can be until I encountered this artwork. It awed me and touched my soul.

Table and Chairs

In the Broad Collection museum in Los Angeles, there is a Robert Therrien sculpture. It consists of a huge table accompanied by four chairs. The table is so big that adults could easily walk under it. When I walked in the room where it is displayed, I felt like a child again. A rush of joy washed over me. I felt a sense of intrigue being under the table, like a young child hiding from an older brother or sister. I also wanted to climb on the chairs, just as a child might. The encounter with these gigantic pieces of furniture made me feel small and a bit helpless. But it also provided a joyous sense of delight along with fear in their oversized proportions; almost like some menacing giant lived there.

—Allen Klein

Advanced Technology

AWE FACTOR: ASTONISHING

When I was growing up, JFK airport wasn't even built yet. The major New York City air terminal was LaGuardia. Most people we knew never traveled by plane except for my cousin Bernice. She was a world traveler. At least once a year, sometimes more often, she would get on a plane to some remote destination.

I remember going to LaGuardia Airport to see her off. It is hard to image but back then it was a thrill to watch a plane take off. The airport even had an observation deck to facilitate the viewing.

I was in awe seeing the plane sitting on the runway with its propellers turning. My cousin always sat near the window so that we could wave to each other as she took off. It was thrilling seeing the plane taxi down the runway and rise into the sky.

I'm not as awed by planes today as I was then, but they still amaze me. Hundreds of people eating dinner or watching a movie in a long metal tube that weighs thousands of pounds and traveling at hundreds of miles an hour above the clouds.

In discussing awe, it may seem absurd to compare the majesty of Grand Canyon to the efficiency of a jumbo jet or an Apple computer, and yet there is a certain wonder in all things tech. There is wonder in the fact that I can have breakfast in the morning in San Francisco and dinner that same night in New York City. That I don't have to cut-and-paste to write my books anymore. That I can have a virtual birthday party with friends who live halfway around the world.

Space Travel

AWE FACTOR: MIND-BOGGLING

Every now and then something comes along that captures the world's imagination and provides a sense of awe and wonder. Space exploration and putting a man on the moon did that. As author Ray Bradbury noted, "Space travel has made children of us all again."

Space travel awed us because it provided a sense of accomplishment and a chance to see people with incredible courage. It showed us things like men walking on the moon that we previously only saw in movies. Now it was a reality.

And we got see the magnificence of earth, even vicariously, in a new way. For example, astronaut James Irwin revealed that "the earth reminded us of a Christmas tree ornament hanging in the blackness of space. As we got farther and farther away it diminished in size. Finally, it shrank to the size of a marble, the most beautiful marble you can imagine."

Angel of Light

[Sitting in a lecture hall at Harvard,] someone stood up in class and said, "Dr. Tillich, in three minutes the Russian Sputnik satellite will come into view in the skies over Cambridge." We all filed out onto the steps, craned our necks upward, and waited for the appearance of the new star. In awe, we watched this new angel of light come into view and silently traverse the dome of heaven, announcing the coming of the Space Age.

—Sam Keen, *Hymns to an Unknown God*

THE GIFTS OF AWE

Genuine awe connects us with the world in a new way.

—Sharon Salzberg, *Real Love*

"Awe is often thought of as the Gucci handbag of emotions," says Michelle Shiota, an associate professor at Arizona State University. "It's nice if you can afford one, but that handbag is not something people actually need."

What Shiota is saying is that over the years the study of awe has taken a back seat to other emotions. But that has changed as researchers, including Shiota, are discovering the many benefits awe provides.

The recent surge in awe research primarily started in 2003 with the publication of a paper by psychologists Dacher Keltner of the University of California, Berkeley, and Jonathan Haidt of New York University. The scholarly paper—"Approaching Awe, a Moral, Spiritual and Aesthetic Emotion"—showed how awe works and the effects it has on us. They found that awe consists of two main qualities: perceived vastness (perceiving something to be greater than ourselves) and its ability to challenge or alter our understanding of the world.

For years, Keltner's focus was on the science of happiness. More recently, at the Greater Good Science Center, where he is the director, he has expanded his attention to include wonder and awe in his work.

Recently, I heard Keltner discussing some of his findings, some anecdotal, some scientific. He talked about the benefits of awe in nature. One researcher he mentioned conducted a study with seniors, who are more likely to be depressed and anxious than the rest of the population. The group was taken on daily "awe walks," where they were instructed to find a spot that might give them awe—a tree, a swing, a beautiful part of the city, etc. After eight weeks the seniors reported being less depressed. In addition, the more the participants took part in the awe walks over time, the more they found things that awed them.

An important point that Keltner related was that we don't need "took-my-breath-away" experiences to benefit from awe moments. Little bursts of awe on a regular basis can make a big difference.

WHY IS AWE IMPORTANT?

As I mentioned in the beginning of the book, I am not a scientist, so I won't go into detail of the past and current research being done in the field. But I am very grateful for these researchers and scientists who are advancing our knowledge of this important emotion.

And for those scientific minds who want to know more, they can see below some of the research on awe, along with what that research found about the benefits of awe.

Research Paper:

Awe Expands People's Perception of Time, Alters Decisions-Making, and Enhances Well-Being (Rudd, et al., 2012, *Studies 2 and 3*)

Awe Expands Our Sense of Time

When we access awe, we perceive time as expansive, and when we see time this way, we are more present, have more patience, and more likely to volunteer our time.

Awe Decreases Materialism

Participants in the Greater Good Science Center study more strongly preferred experiences over material goods. According to center, "The experience of awe elevates people from their mundane concerns, which are bounded by daily experiences such as the desire for money."

Awe Increases Life Satisfaction

Participants in the study reported that reflecting on awe resulted in significantly increased mood boosts and life satisfaction.

Research Paper:

Awe, the Small Self, and Prosocial Behavior (Piff et al., 2015, Study 4)

Awe Encourages Compassion

An awe experience directs our attention away from our own benefit and toward the greater good.

Research Paper:

Awe's effects on generosity and helping. (Prade & Saroglou, 2016)

Awe Increases Generosity

Participants were asked to imagine winning the lottery. Those who reflected on awe-inspiring experiences were significantly more generous with sharing their potential winnings than those who reflected on neural ones.

Research Paper:

Awe in nature heals: Evidence from military veterans, at-risk youth, and college students. (Anderson, et al., 2018)

Awe Contributes to Well-Being

This study showed the impact of nature had on well-being and the decrease of stress-related symptoms.

Research Papers:

Awe, the diminished self, and collective engagement: Universals and cultural variations in the small self. (Bai, et al., 2017)

The nature of awe: Elicitors, appraisals, and effects on self-concept (Shiota & Keltner, 2007, Study 4)

Awe Connects Us to Others

Increases the awareness that we are part of something bigger and provides greater feelings of closeness with others and humanity.

Small Self

While we're feeling small in an awe moment, we are feeling connected to more people or feeling closer to others. That's awe's purpose, or at least one of its purposes.

**—Yang Bai, associate professor,
University of California, Berkeley**

Positive effect and markers of inflammation: discrete positive emotions predict lower levels of inflammatory cytokines. (Stellar, et al., 2015, Study 2)

Awe Reduces Inflammation

Those who experienced more awe, wonder and amazement, had lower levels of Interleukin 6, a marker of inflammation.

Awe and humility. (Stellar, et al., 2017)

Awe Increases Humility

Those who were more prone to experiencing awe were found to be less self-absorbed, less narcissistic and more humble.

Teaching creativity to children from a galaxy away. (Liberman, et al., 2012)

Awe Sparks Creativity

"Expansive thinking," as in awe moments, can lead to increased creativity. Awe helps us see things in a new light.

An exploratory study into the effects of extraordinary nature on emotions, mood, and prosociality. (Joye & Bolderdijk, 2015)

Awe Enhances Positive Emotions

Even without actually being in nature, awe improved a person's mood after watching a slideshow of awe-inspiring nature scenes.

Other studies have shown that awe tends to bring us into the present moment, lower our stress levels, and make us more curious. We all know how wonderful it is when we experience an awe moment that is not associated with fear. It will be up to researchers to continue to show us the positive benefits of awe.

THAT'S
AWESOME

Cleveland fans are awesome.

—LeBron James

Dancing with the Stars is awesome.

—Sabrina Bryan

Some people think I am gay, which I think is awesome.

—Daniel Radcliffe

It is hard to imagine writing a book on the subject of awe without mentioning one of the most overused words in the English language these days. That word, of course, is *awesome*. So, to end this section of the book, I close with some awesome thoughts on the word awesome.

In her humorous TED talk, "Please, please, people. Let's put the 'awe' back in 'awesome,' " Jill Shargaa pokes fun at *awesome*.

She says that when she was dining at a café recently, the server came over to the table and asked if they had eaten there before. Shargaa replied, "Yes, yes we have." And the server replied, "Awesome!"

"Really?" she thought. "Awesome? Or merely good that we've decided to visit your restaurant again?"

Shargaa continues, "The other day a coworker asked if I could save a file as a pdf. And I said, 'Well, of course.' And as she said 'Awesome!' I thought 'Seriously, can saving anything as a pdf be awesome?' "

Shargaa points to the dictionary definition of awesome which is fear mingled with admiration or reverence, a feeling produced by something majestic. "With that in mind," she sarcastically asks, "Was your Quiznos sandwich *awesome*? How about that parking space—was that *awesome*? Or the game the other day, was that *awesome*?"

The answer, she says, is, "No. No. And no. The sandwich can be delicious. The parking space can be nearby. And the game can be a blowout." But she emphasizes, "Not everything can be *awesome*!"

God Is No Longer Awesome

A few years ago, the *New York Times* published a story about a prayer book, used by conservative Jews during the High Holy Days. It said that, because of the overuse of the word awesome, the book will no longer use the word "awesome" to describe God. "The word, which has become an all-purpose exclamation that spread from Valley Girls to much of American teenagerdom," the *Times* stated, "has lost its spiritual punch and dignity..."

"The authors prefer 'awe-inspiring' " the article said.

The rabbi who headed the committee, which wrote and translated the new book, noted that, "If you say God is awesome, you are immediately in street language, rather than inspiring language."

And finally, in his blog, comedian Greg Schwem jokes about the current overuse of the word "awesome":

Consider a recent day in my life: It began with a cycling class at my health club. My instructor labeled the early morning turnout awesome. As we labored through forty-five minutes of inclines and speed training, three times our efforts were deemed awesome. When class concluded, we were asked to clean our bikes using the nearby antibacterial wipes.

"That would be awesome," the instructor said. From there I was off to the airport for a flight to Miami. "How's it going today?" the flight attendant inquired as I boarded.

I refused to pad the numbers in my own experiment. "Breathtaking," I said. "Awesome," she replied.

It only got worse from there. "Did you want cream in your coffee?" asked a second, male flight attendant when taking my drink order.

"Nope. Just black," I said.

"Awesome."

I smugly looked at my seatmate, who requested cream and, therefore, did not receive the accolades bestowed upon me.

"What brings you to Miami?" I asked.

"Heading home," he replied. "You?"

"Business."

"What's your business?"

"I'm a comedian."

"For real?" he asked. "That is so awesome."

I slurped my coffee. Loudly.

Upon landing in Miami, I retrieved my bag and located my driver for the thirty-minute ride to the hotel.

"How was your flight?" he asked.

"Awesome," I said, beating him to the punch.

Schwem reports, "I didn't count that usage in my figures. Still, by two in the afternoon, I had tallied twenty-three utterances of the word."

PART TWO

AWE-INSPIRING STORIES

I think...about bringing that sense of awe into the little things we often take for granted or consider part of the background of our lives. This includes the flowers on the side of the road; the taste of ice cream in our mouths; how groovy it is to suck on a straw and get milk in your mouth; and to find a really, really good stick on the ground. And it is also includes things we generally don't even think of as pleasures, like the warm soapy water on our hands as we washed the dishes.

—Danya Ruttenberg, *Nurture the Wow*

Sometimes you experience an awe moment that not only blows you away, but forever changes your life. Those don't happen very often. More likely, there are either mini awe moments that pass by so quickly you might not recognize them as such. Or, sometimes you have more significant awe moments when you realize that something special, something out of the ordinary, has happened but are hard pressed to explain it.

MINI AWE MOMENTS

CHANCE-MEETING AWE

We are wonderstruck when we're caught off guard by some amazing or surprising thing or person. Unlike being lightning-struck—which is lethal—being wonderstruck is life-giving and spirit-arousing.

—Edward Hays, *A Book of Wonders*

Meeting on Top of the World

Several years ago, I went hiking in Yosemite National Park with my husband. We were near the top of the Mist Trail which leads to the magnificent Vernal Falls. As we approached the summit, someone who was headed down the trail shouted out my name. The voice was familiar, but I had a hard time recognizing the person's face. It wasn't until I got closer that I could tell who it was. He was an apprentice of mine in summer stock when I was a scenic designer. It was probably at least thirty-five years since we had seen each other and here we were, meeting again in the most unlikely of places.

Meeting across the World

Another time, my husband and I were vacationing in Paris. It was a long flight from San Francisco, so the first thing we did when we got to our hotel was take a short nap. We then headed for a walk in the sunshine to reset our internal time clock. When we turned our first corner, there was a friend from San Francisco sipping coffee in a café. Neither of us had known we would be in Paris at the same time.

Meeting at the Airport

A few years ago, I was at the airport waiting for my flight to Newark, New Jersey. Seated next to me was a couple who were going to London. They were very upset because their flight had a long delay which meant that they would miss a show for which they had tickets on the day they arrived.

I chatted with them awhile, gave them a card about my latest book, *You Can't Ruin My Day*, and reminded them of how a child might see this as an adventure. I encouraged them to focus on the things that were right rather than the things that weren't.

Fast-forward to almost a year later during the intermission of a show in San Francisco where I live. A man came over to me and asked if I was Allen Klein. Then he told me that we last saw each other when his flight to London was delayed. He wanted to thank me for the advice I gave him. He said that my "you-can't-ruin-my-day" philosophy helped make him and his wife's trip remarkable. Moreover, because their flight was delayed so long, the airline put them on an earlier flight that got them to London in time to see the show.

I often call these awesome incidents "mini miracles." I mean what were the chances that a man I met many months ago and I would be seeing the same show on the same night clear across the country from where we first met and that he would spot me among the thousand or so people in the theater?

CHANCE-HAPPENING AWE

Wonder and awe allow us to transcend the ordinary.

—Louie Schwartzberg, on MovingArt.com

Twenty-One

I borrowed a book from the library and read as far as page twenty-one. Because I liked the book and wanted to have a copy in my library, I order it online. It arrived yesterday with the jacket flap tucked in at page twenty-one.

The Brain Surgeon

Two weeks ago, I accompanied my friend to the hospital. She had a couple of episodes of vertigo and her MRI revealed an aneurysm near her brain. Her doctor thought it nothing to worry about but made an appointment with the head brain surgeon at a medical center near me to check it out.

As expected, she was extremely nervous about the appointment. I offered to go with her for support. At first she refused, but then as the date got closer, she asked if I would join her. And I'm glad I did. I provided someone she could talk to and distract her from her anxiety while she waited to be called to the exam room. I could also be a second ear to hear the diagnosis. But perhaps the one thing we hadn't counted on was that I also was the foil for any laughter that might arise...and it did.

In the exam room, a doctor greeted us who looked like he was straight out of central casting—young, handsome, clean-cut. His outfit was perfect too—white starched medical jacket with his name embroidered on the right side, polished shoes, and a starched white shirt and neatly knotted silk tie.

He went through all of my friend's exam results, asked her several questions, then declared, to our relief, that there was no need to worry. The aneurysm should probably be checked yearly but wasn't anything to be concerned about. If it did rupture, which was extremely rare, it would not cause damage to the brain.

The young doctor then told us he would be sending in the chief brain surgeon who would basically repeat what we had just been told. That is where the laughter began.

When the principal surgeon entered the room, my friend and I looked at each other in amazement. Unlike the previous doctor, he looked more like a cross-country truck driver. Big, tall, and muscular. Instead of a starched white doctor's coat, he was dressed in an extremely wrinkled gray-blue jacket with pants of a different color and very much disheveled. His hair was uncombed, and he needed a shave. Perhaps he was up all-night operating? Partying? Driving across the country?

I sat there thinking that maybe central casting sent him to the wrong room. Maybe someone in costumes gave him the wrong outfit. Maybe he was supposed to go to the shipping department. But no. He was the head brain surgeon. He knew what he was talking about. He explained my friend's situation and comforted all of her concerns. He was, although he didn't look it, the real thing.

I tell you this because there is more to the story, a related part two with a surprisingly mini awe moment.

Two days ago, I was coming back to my house after walking the dog. A large station wagon-like car had just pulled up in front. A couple got out and the man, seeing me open the gate, asked if I lived there. I replied that I did. He wanted to make sure he was not in my driveway and whether it was OK to park overnight. He had just driven down to San Francisco from near Yosemite, where he lived. He said that the hospital, where he was going to have an operation the next day, had put him up for the night at the hotel around the corner.

I told him that it was fine to park there as long as he moved the car by noon the next day when the streets would be cleaned. I also wished him well and asked where the surgery would take place. He told me that it would be at same hospital where I had accompanied my friend.

I then asked what kind of operation he was having. He said matter-of-factly, "brain surgery."

***

While the story above is only about a small awe moment, incidents like this one, which some people might attribute to coincidence, always amaze me. Particularly because in order for this to happen a number of things had to occur within seconds of each other or there would have been no awe moment.

After all, there was a strong chance that I might not have accompanied my friend to the doctor's office in the hospital or that she might have gone to a different one. And the same is true of the man from Yosemite. He could have parked anywhere in the neighborhood. In addition, I could have come back from walking the dog a minute or two earlier, or later, and totally missed him. If he looked the other way for a few seconds he might not have seen me entering my house.

Moreover, when we did meet, our brief conversation could have only involved his parking space. He might not have said anything about an operation or where the procedure would take place. Nor, without me asking about what kind of operation he would be having, would he have revealed that it would be brain surgery.

I'll never know which surgeon operated on him, whether it was the one I met or not. But certainly, as the head brain surgeon in the hospital, there is a very good chance that the two of them connected via hospital charts or even in person.

Rental Car

When I was four years old and watching Tonto and the Lone Ranger on television helping people in distress, I decided I wanted to do healing work. Not like being a doctor or a nurse. I wanted to do what some people these days would call the "woo-woo" kind—doing some good for someone who needed some healing.

Jump ahead many years later. I'm studying about such things as laying on of hands, prayer, acupressure, acupuncture, etc. I got this image in my head of riding a horse in the country, not that I could actually ride a horse, and in my saddlebag I would have just about anything anyone would need to be healed—herbal tea, injection needles, acupressure cards.

Then life took over, so I let my idea go. I got married. I got divorced. Then I needed a job. So, I became a nurse where I needed to keep my dream of alternative healing on the down-low. I started out doing regular nursing, then, after a couple of years, switched to home nursing.

One day I'm driving to a patient's house in the country thinking, "Isn't this the dream I had years ago?" I look down at the passenger's seat. There were a couple of syringes, an acupressure card, some herbal teas, and my stethoscope. And I'm thinking, this is indeed like the dream I had, minus the horse.

Then I realized what a WOW moment it was when I looked down at the name of my rental car. It was a Dodge Colt!

—Debra Joy Hart

My friend, and very talented composer, David Friedman, shared this mini awe moment:

Recently, I was talking to my Al-Anon sponsor on the phone, and I was very upset about something, can't even remember what. And she said, "David, I want to read you something that I think might be helpful." She went and got a book and read me an amazing passage that was perfect for what I was going through. And I said, "That was amazing. It was brilliant. It was just what I needed to hear. What book was that from?" And she said, "Oh, it's from this book called *The Thought Exchange* by David Friedman."

Good Evening, Mr. Klein

On the surface it may not have seemed like an awe moment to most people, but to me it was the awesome recognition of the Divine in all of us.

One evening I went to Feinstein's nightclub in San Francisco. They have wonderful cabaret acts, many of whom have performed on Broadway. Being a fan of Broadway musicals, I'm always delighted to see and hear these multi-talented performers in person, especially in such an intimate setting.

The venue has no pre-selected seating. Instead a maître d' escorts you to a table upon your arrival. On my recent visit, the person who is usually at the front desk was seating other patrons, so someone else took us to our seats. As we were walking down the entryway to our table, we passed the regular front desk person. And she warmly greeted me, "Good evening, Mr. Klein."

I was surprised that she remembered my name. After all, I only attend these shows on an occasional basis, perhaps once every few months. I was delighted that she remembered who I was. It made my evening extra special.

After the show, I thought about this fleeting incident and realized that, for me, it was a tiny awe moment. As in some bigger awe experiences, it was unexpected, contained delight, and on some level represented something bigger— our connection to all humanity.

LOOKING-FOR-A-SIGN AWE

If you are looking for a sign, this is it.

—Anonymous (wording on an actual sign)

When I need to make a significant decision, or even a less important one, I look for a sign—something that will assure me that the decision I am making is the right one. It's usually an accurate indication of how I should proceed. I don't know why it works but most of the time it does. As you can see from the stories below, apparently, I am not the only one to do this.

Twenty-Two

My lucky number is twenty-two. We named my daughter, Althea, after her great-grandmother, but that Althea was called Honey by the family. Toward the end of my pregnancy, we had a scare. Baby Althea was suddenly measuring very small on the ultrasound. The doctor was concerned that she had stopped growing and they wanted me to come back for a high-res ultrasound that afternoon. We spent a very nervous few hours in between appointments, but when we pulled into the hospital parking lot, my fears were put to rest. We were behind a car with the license plate "Honey♥22."

I cried tears of gratitude knowing that no matter what, everything was going to be fine.

—Jessica Raaum Foster

Yellow Rose of Paris

Before I even learned to talk, whenever my maternal grandfather visited us, I would run for my mini-suitcase and thrust it at my mom to pack—in anticipation of going home to my grandparent's neighboring West Texas town with him. As a child, everyone knew "Pappy" and I were inseparable.

In my adolescence, Pappy called me a long-stem rose, even though I was only long-stemmed. He always crooned "The Yellow Rose of Texas" to me, too, but our closeness dissipated somewhat when I developed into a young woman. In the late '90s, as a new mother and wife, I moved to Paris with my husband about the same time Pappy began his decline with dementia. The last time I visited him, he knew I was someone he liked but wasn't quite sure whom.

He died in late January of 2003. Distraught, I flew to West Texas for the funeral and then back to Paris only to learn that the NASA Space Shuttle *Challenger* had exploded and rained debris all across my home state. It was an apt metaphor for my feelings. Not only had I failed to be there for him at the end, but I felt that he would never know how much his unconditional love had meant and the strength it had given me throughout my life. I longed for a sign to know that Pap was at peace.

Two days later, I was walking to the Metro deep in thought. The neighborhood eccentric who rummaged through garbage bins approached, inexplicably carrying an armful of flowers. As he jogged past, a yellow rose dropped at my feet.

Thank you, Pappy.

—Ann Jacobus, author

Italy or Not Italy?

I remember trying to decide whether or not to go to Italy and asked for a sign. The next street I crossed was Florence Avenue. Yep. A real sign was the sign.

—Ann Licater

MAJOR AWE MOMENTS

HIGHER-POWER AWE

God intentionally loaded the world with amazing things to leave you astounded. The air-conditioned termite mound in Africa, the tart crunchiness of an apple, the explosion of thunder, the beauty of an orchid, the interdependent systems of the human body, the inexhaustible pounding of the ocean waves, and thousands of other created sights, sounds, touches, and tastes—God designed all to be awesome. And he intended you to be daily amazed.

—Paul David Tripp, *Awe: Why It Matters for Everything We Think, Say, & Do*

Awe often connects us to some higher power, something grander than our daily existence on earth. In fact, many people connect life-changing awe moments with a religious experience. Yes, awe can stem from an encounter with God, although an encounter with nature is the most frequent awe trigger.

A friend of mine, who believes that awe needs a religious connection, said that my view of awe—of seeing it all around us—is more a reflection of my view of life rather than that of a definition of awe. She might be right but, from the interviews I've done, a lot of people define awe with a similarly broad view.

Another friend, Jim Oerther, did have an awe experience of Jesus coming to him. As a result, he enrolled in seminary.

But he also notes that it is not necessarily the earth-shattering experiences but the things that happen to us every day that we need to recognize. Oerther makes an important point. He says, "It's not even seeing a glorious sunset in some national park someplace, even if you don't have a direct line to the sunset, sometimes it's just seeing the pink haze in the sky reflecting on the clouds or seeing the sunset in a window."

So maybe it is not important if it is mini or major awe. But more importantly, as psychologist Abraham Maslow reminds us, they all might be intertwined: "The great lesson from the true mystics...is that the sacred is in the ordinary, that it is to be found in one's daily life, in one's neighbors, friends, and family, in one's backyard."

A Gift from God

Last evening, I attended a class in which we were discussing the connection between giving and taking. During the discussion, a disheveled young man entered the room. Both the teacher and Robert, a student in the class, went to see who he was and what he wanted. The teacher came back to continue teaching the class while Robert continued to interact with the stranger. At one point, they both left the building. About ten minutes later Robert came back and told a remarkable story of what happened.

It seems the unkempt stranger was walking the streets hoping to find some solace in a church. But, being nighttime, they were all closed. He passed our spiritual center, Unity San Francisco, and walked in thinking we were having a service. In chatting with him, Robert found out that he needed eighteen dollars to get to Fresno where he said he could get some sort of housing. He stated that a check was being sent there for some work he had done but he couldn't get it until he checked into his living quarters.

Like many of us may feel when someone asks for a handout, Robert initially felt that he was being taken. Maybe this hardship story wasn't true at all. Maybe he didn't really need the money. Maybe he repeats this same woe-is-me story to a lot of people.

Nevertheless, Robert didn't listen to those negative thoughts, especially after the class was just discussing *inner-centered* giving which involves giving without expecting anything in return. After much trouble getting the ATM machine across the street to work, Robert withdrew twenty dollars. He gave it to the young man who went on his way.

When Robert returned, the class found a number of remarkable things in what happened. Among them was that the young man, who could have asked for any amount of money, only requested eighteen dollars. What is so amazing is that in the Jewish tradition, the number eighteen, *chai* in Hebrew, is the word for "life." And in its plural form, *chaim*, is often used in a toast, *l'chaim*, meaning "to life."

Robert also told us that the man's name was Matthew, one of the twelve apostles whose name means "gift of God."

The appearance of this man just as we were discussing the act of giving, and all of its ramifications, seemed so impeccably timed that we joked with the teacher about his having hired an actor to provide the perfect illustration for the lesson. Of course, that wasn't true, but it provided a bit of levity to what seemed like a somewhat mysterious occurrence.

After the class, I kept wondering if this was a scam or not. When I got back home, I checked to see if there was a train from San Francisco to Fresno at one-fifteen in the morning, the time Matthew said it would be leaving. There wasn't. And, in addition, there wasn't any train either during the daytime or at night that cost anywhere near eighteen dollars.

So, who knows if Matthew was telling the truth or not? But somehow it didn't matter. It was a very small price to pay for such a great example of giving. And who knows, maybe he was indeed a gift from God.

A Gift That God Gave Me

In the Broadway musical *Billy Elliot*, one of the judges auditioning the young ballet dancer asks him, "What does it feel like when you're dancing?" Elliot responds that he hasn't got the words to describe it. So instead of words, he provides images in song. He sings that when he's dancing it's like he's flying, flying like a bird—like electricity.

That is similar to what Michele Spitz (womanofherword. com) told me about her once-in-a-lifetime awe moment. She says, "It was like a surge of electricity running through my body. It was amazing. The most euphoric experience of my whole life."

For more than twenty-five years, Spitz had a career in the real estate marketing industry. Her true passion, however, was in philanthropy and supporting the disabled, senior, and underserved communities in the arts.

One day, out of the blue, she was given the opportunity to narrate a full-length film. It was produced by two visually impaired brothers and specifically created for low-vision and blind audiences. It was something Spitz had never done before.

After completing the project, she exited the studio and was suddenly stopped in her tracks. Like Billy Elliot, she was electrified. "I can't believe I did this project," she recalls. "I can't believe I was in the recording studio for four hours straight. I can't believe I was capable of this voice-over art form." Suddenly she got a realization that her powerful voice was the perfect match for this kind of work.

So, Spitz's new career began—narrating museum, digital media, and film content for the visually impaired. "It has been the happiest time of my life," she says. In spite of the fact that she obtained a college degree in broadcasting and yet had never pursued a career in this field, her awe moment revealed exactly why she was put on this planet—"to be the voice for the eyes that can't see."

She describes her career in audio description (the service that makes media accessible for people with vision loss) as "the gift that God gave me." By the happenstance of being at the right place at the right moment, her time, talent, and treasure came together in one glorious package. And Spitz is most grateful for it all.

She concludes, "What an honor and a gift is it for me to have been given this unique opportunity to help so many people experience the arts in ways that were not possible years ago."

A Gift from Beyond

Several years ago, my husband Dave and I attended a retreat at Unity Village in Kansas City. During one of the days there, each of us had a few unscheduled hours to do whatever we chose. He went for a long walk and I signed up to attend an Akashic records workshop. The Akashic records are said to be a compilation of all human events, thoughts, words, emotions, and intent ever to have occurred in the past, present, or future.

The instructor guided us in a mediation and asked us to sit quietly for a while before proceeding. Then she instructed us to ask someone from the past a question. That being would then channel their answer to us. After some time, I asked my deceased wife a question about why she died at such a young age leaving me alone with our ten-year-old daughter. Her answer surprised me and brought tears to my eyes.

She told me all would be all right...her part was complete and that it was mine to carry forward now. She told me not to worry, "I sent Dave to take care of you."

After the class, I walked slowly across the campus thinking about her answer. I went down the stairs that led to the dining room and alongside the long outdoor corridor of the temple building. Just as I turned the corner, there was Dave coming toward me. Sobbing, I embraced him and told him what had just happened. And there we stood on this spiritual ground—awed with a greater understanding of a Divine presence.

Answered Prayers

Herb Felsenfeld, from San Francisco, California, shared this awe story about his son, Nathan Zev. When Nathan was in the middle of a Columbia University graduate internship, he contracted a serious gastrointestinal illness. Felsenfeld's brother also had severe problems with his own GI tract. That, along with his own weakened condition, led Nathan to question if his college education was doomed and if he would ever be able to continue with his passion for public affairs.

When things got worse, Felsenfeld and his wife flew across country to be with their son. They took a room in West Harlem, which was within walking distance of their son's apartment. During their stay, there was no progress in Nathan's disease. He didn't improve; he didn't get worse.

As a believer in the power of prayer, Felsenfeld looked for nearby houses of worship. He found two: The Cathedral of St. John the Divine, and the Riverside Church. He took his wife Gail to the Cathedral, but coming from a very strong, culturally Jewish background, she felt uncomfortable there.

Alone, Felsenfeld walked to the Riverside Church. He joined an existing prayer group. The congregants responded with voices that shook the rafters. The woman in charge of the group led devotions that lasted almost an hour. Real "prayer-warriors," Felsenfeld thought as the parishioners filled the room with positive prayers and thoughts for his son.

The next days were filled with more tests and the anxiety of waiting for the results from the GI specialist. Then, one night, during dinner at his son's house, the sound of the telephone broke the silence. Nathan, with the phone to his ear, was quietly pacing the room. He kept repeating, "... normal." And again, "Normal." He thanked the doctor and switched off his cell.

Joyfully he cried out, "My tests are normal. Mom, Dad, my tests are normal!" The three hugged with tears welling up in their eyes.

***

Earlier in the interview Felsenfeld said, "Awe is what amazes and astounds me." The power of prayer met that criteria. "Although I'm the only one in the family who believes it," he says, "I felt my prayers worked. This awe-filled moment was unforgettable."

Spirituality at the Pyramids

My friend Jim Gebbie is a travel writer. He has had many awe moments on his adventures around the world. When I asked him what his greatest one was, he told me this story about the great pyramids.

> I had been a skeptic most of my life until I had a private setback, which deeply affected me. Since then I have been seeking to learn more about a Higher Power—and myself.

> My readings had taken me from scholarly, inspirational works to Benjamin Hoff's *The Tao of Pooh*, a lighthearted look at Eastern philosophy. What better place to look for the mystical, I thought, than in Egypt, the land of the pharaohs? Winnie the Pooh was to be my paperback traveling companion.

On the morning I left California, I asked myself, "Will I find the spirituality I seek there?" Immediately an inner voice said, "If you *look*, you will find it."

Because of jetlag, I awoke around one in the morning. I dressed and went to the coffee shop for a light meal and a chapter of Pooh. Since I was wide awake, I thought I would wander up El Ahram Street to the pyramids.

A young Egyptian soldier stopped me at the darkened entrance. In halting English, he said the pyramids were closed. I didn't want to leave, and after a short conversation I suggested I might pay him something— which he accepted.

My initial view was pitch-black except for a few streetlights. I could see the lights of Cairo in the distance and then a gigantic mountain of stone blocks loomed in the lamplight before me. It was the Great Pyramid.

The pyramid was every bit as large—every bit as awesome—as I had imagined it.

Alone, I walked toward Chephren's Pyramid and climbed up a course or two of the chest-high stones that formed the base.

It was an awe-inspiring moment. I knew this was where I was supposed to be. I said a prayer and knew that a Power greater than myself was there. I had a strange urge: I moistened my finger with saliva and rubbed the drop of wetness on the rough, ancient stone. It was my offering, my mark, my connection with the ancient past.

In awe I felt the power of the pyramids and of my Higher Power. I felt the ancientness of these rocky pinnacles that had been erected nearly five thousand years ago, and I knew they were young as I looked up at the cold white stars. I felt a part of the entire universe and that God was everywhere. And my inner voice said: "This is only the beginning."

CONNECTED-TO-THE-UNIVERSE AWE

I have been ambushed by the power of the moon, held captive by fireflies dancing at dusk, bowled over by wobbly white shoots beneath a rock pushing their way out to life, moved to tears by the sight of a small finch falling from the roof. I have lain on the picnic table and gazed at the stars in sheer ecstasy.

—Joyce Rupp, *The Cosmic Dance*

Magical Waters

"Awe is hard to explain," says Janice Holly Booth, author of *Only Pack What You Can Carry.* "It is that feeling of being part of something so immense, yet so granular all at the same time, where the interconnection to the vast web of life and all its mysteries reveals itself for a moment."

Booth explains, "In that moment of awe, I am no longer a human body standing on the ground or swimming in the ocean, but a collection of molecules interacting with all the other molecules around me, sharing air and water and a profound sense of oneness."

To vividly illustrate her definition, she provided this example:

I was snorkeling in the Galapagos Islands. The water was very cold, and rough. As I was making the decision to return to the boat, a giant sea turtle swam beneath me and hung out there for a little while, almost as if to say, "It's OK, don't go."

He then rose right in front of me and started swimming slowly enough that I could follow him. He led me straight to a "field" of marine iguanas feeding on algae underwater. I had to fight the waves to stay with the iguanas, but it was worth it. And when one big wave practically threw me into one of the iguanas, he swam right up to my mask, blew some bubbles and then swam off. He looked exactly like a miniature Godzilla. It was incredible!

As if it couldn't get any better, as I was swimming back to the boat, exhausted and freezing, two sea lions came to play. They began swimming around me in circles, doing backflips in the water, and blowing bubbles at my mask.

When I got back in the boat, I looked out over the churning ocean and thought how much magic lives beneath the skin of that water. And how, for just a moment, I was connected to it all.

Something Greater

My friend Robert Kane is an avid open-water swimmer. Since he lives near San Francisco, he has access to the natural body of water surrounding that city. One day he was with a group that swam across the span under the Golden Gate Bridge. He notes that it is one of the deepest sections of the bay with a lot of strange currents, waves, and swells.

Kane remembers the boat he was in getting closer and closer to the massive towers that support the bridge. Looking up under the bridge it dawned on him that he never really comprehended its enormity. Just then the swim director said to get in the cold fifty-six-degree water. After adjusting to the churning water, he got his stride. He saw the bridge on one side and the vast ocean on the other. "The next stop perhaps leading to China, or something like that?" he says.

With such vastness, Kane notes that one part of him felt small, insignificant. But the other part of him felt like he "meshed into something so much bigger."

"All of a sudden, it wasn't just me as a person in the water. It was me as part of the planet...the tidal currents, the ocean, the manmade structures that we build to navigate them. I just started to get a connection of what it took to build the bridge, what it took for nature to build these mountains and everything that was around me."

Kane concludes, "The experience is indescribable. In some ways I would say it was ecstatic. I felt more alive than I could ever remember feeling. It was just that feeling of being part of that vast expanse of everything. And that is why I would consider it an awe moment."

Time Stopped

Dave Baron had a similar experience to Kane's when viewing a total eclipse of the sun. In his TED talk about it, he describes his first eclipse moment and how awe-inspiring it was. "For the first time in my life," he says, "I felt viscerally connected to the universe in all its enormity." He adds, "Time stopped. Or it was nonexistent."

Baron was so moved by this experience that he now travels the world to view as many total eclipses as he can whenever and wherever they happen.

Time Stands Still

I step out of the house for a quick walk... I am no more than three minutes into a brisk pace when I pass a creek in the ravine. It beckons to me. I stop, undecided for a moment whether to let myself enjoy this peaceful spot, or to walk on and get my exercise. The creek wins... The sounds draw me in until I am no longer aware of sitting by the creek. I later realize I have to check my watch. I'm startled to find that a half hour has gone by, and it's time to go. It's hard to leave. I feel as if I am being held. A sweet fullness lingers all afternoon and lasts for days. Something has happened... Two years have passed, and I still wonder about the magic that afternoon.

—**Anne Scott,** *Serving Fire*

Something Special

One day, I was watching a father hold his just-turned-one-year-old. The boy was facing outward and enthralled by everything that came his way. When someone came toward him, he lit up with a great big smile. When his father moved his hand in front of the child, the one-year-old smiled again joyfully trying to grab it. When there was a noise nearby, it brought another smile to the child's face.

Everything awed him. Even ordinary, everyday things were a new discovery for him.

What I got to witness was what Zen Buddhism labels as "seeing the world with a beginner's mind." And we don't need to be a one-year-old to find the awe in the world. In *Secrets Kids Know...That Adults Oughta Learn*, I write about a retired schoolteacher who I saw on a television show years ago. She took young children on hikes on the hills near San Francisco.

What was so unusual about the outings was the way she delighted in a childlike sense of discovery. She would frequently stop to point out what she called "something special" to the kids. A ladybug: "Look, something special." An orange poppy: "Look, something special." The dew on a blade of grass: "Look, something special." Even a plain gray rock or an ordinary weed was special.

Of course, the roles could have been reversed and the kids could have easily shown the elderly lady all of the things around them that were indeed "special" because they often see the world with fresh eyes. But the TV show (which was about people who volunteered) was really for adults who often miss the specialness of seemingly ordinary things. Young kids, on the other hand, often see the wonder in things that grown-ups take for granted.

CONNECTED-TO-OTHERS
AWE

To enter into the presence of another human being is to enter into the presence of God in a new and different way... We must come into the presence of our fellow human beings with a sense of awe and gratitude.

—Stephen L. Carter, *Civility*

Walk in My Shoes

Mary Yonekawa says that one of her awe moments didn't come together until after her father died. "My husband Ron, my son Zack, and I were driving to plan the funeral for my dad. Zack, who was thirteen at the time, was sitting in the back seat and asked, 'Oh Ma, what will our family do without grandpa?' "

In order to tell her son what a wonderful man they were losing, Yonekawa shared that he was not only a dentist but that he devoted his time to numerous organizations. Among them was the school board, of which he was president, and which involved handing out diplomas to graduating junior high students.

At one graduation her father found that one of the students didn't have the proper dress shoes. The powers that be wanted to send the student back home to change his shoes but that would have delayed the graduation. Her father took charge and solved the situation.

"Well," he said, "I'm going to be standing on stage above everyone seated below. They're never going to see my feet." He then took off his shoes and told someone to find the boy and give him the shoes. Mary's father never knew who the boy was.

Many years later, Mary's husband and her father were playing a game of pool in the basement. During the game, both men were sharing some stories. Her father told his shoe story. Then her husband revealed "My most embarrassing moment was the night of my graduation when I didn't have the right shoes."

The Subway Ride

In *Drinking the Rain,* author Alix Kates Shulman writes:

> I was sitting alone on the downtown IRT on my way to pick up the children at their after-school music classes. The train had just pulled out of the Twenty-third Street station and was accelerating to its cruising speed. All around me people sat bundled up in mufflers, damp woolen coats, and slush-stained boots, reading newspapers or staring off blankly as the train jerked along the track...

> Then suddenly the dull light in the car began to shine with exceptional lucidity until everything around me was glowing with an indescribable aura, and I saw in the row of motley passengers opposite the miraculous connection of all living beings. Not felt;

saw. What began as a desultory thought grew to a vision, large and unifying, in which all the people in the car hurtling downtown together, including myself, like all the people on the planet hurtling together around the sun—our entire living cohort—formed one united family, indissolubly connected by the rare and mysterious accident of life. No matter what our countless superficial differences, we were equal, we were one, by virtue of simply being alive at this moment out of all the possible moments stretching endlessly back and ahead. The vision filled me with overwhelming love for the entire human race and a feeling that no matter how incomplete or damaged our lives, we were surpassingly lucky to be alive. Then the train pulled into the station and I got off.

The Clown Nose

For several years in a row, my teenage daughter was a counselor at Camp Tawonga near Yosemite National Park. Every year she would ask me to come and speak to her fellow counselors. They were often stressed out and she thought my talk about using humor to cope might help them lighten up. In the presentation, I do an activity in which every participant gets a clown nose.

Every year I would make some kind of excuse for why I could not do the talk—"I'm too busy, Sarah." "It's a long drive, Sarah." "It's too hot up there in the summer, Sarah." Then one year, while attending my annual speakers' convention, I heard a presenter give a powerful talk. One of the things he said was that teenagers have the highest rate of suicide in this country. His words moved me. I immediately left his presentation, called my daughter, and asked, "When do you want me to come speak to the counselors?"

When I arrived, my daughter had posted a sign on almost every tree at the camp. It had a cartoon drawing of me. Under that it read: "If you see this man, give him a big hug."

When I met up with Sarah, she told me that I would be speaking at eleven o'clock. "OK," I said. "I'll be ready at eleven in the morning." "No Dad," she said, "eleven o'clock at night, after all the campers have gone to bed."

As I started my talk, I scanned the room looking for a friend of Sarah's who was also a counselor. He was very shy and often depressed. I didn't see him in the room at first but during the program I spotted him crouched down behind a couch. His head would bob up every now and then. Whenever our eyes met, he would duck behind the couch again.

Around midnight the talk was over. I searched for Sarah's friend, but he quickly disappeared. Months later I ran into him on Haight Street. Usually he would hardly acknowledge me but this time he immediately came over and was eager to share something.

It seems that the day after my talk, he decided to leave the camp. He wasn't getting along with the other counselors. And since he no longer spoke to his mom or dad, he couldn't go home. So, he decided to hitchhike.

For hours, car after car whizzed by. As each one passed, he said he felt more and more depressed and more and more deserted. As it was getting dark, he started to cry and planned how he was going to kill himself. Then, as he was pulling out a handkerchief from his pocket to wipe away his tears, the clown nose I gave out in my workshop fell on the ground. He said, he bent down to retrieve it and put it on. Immediately someone stopped and gave him a ride.

"Maybe lightening up a bit can get me further than I thought," he said. "Thank you for coming to speak to us— and thank you for saving my life."

The Bookstore

After one of my books was published, I stopped by the Bookshop West Portal, in San Francisco, where my book signing would take place the following evening. I thought I was there to check the AV setup, but something happened that made me believe I was really guided to be there for something else.

When I walked in the store, there was a woman at the counter sobbing uncontrollably. It seemed her husband had died a few days before. When she asked the clerk to recommend a book about grief, somehow his reply upset her. I waited a while to see if she would stop crying or if the clerk would say something to console her. When neither happened, I stepped in.

I shared how I would randomly cry right after my wife died. Never knowing when or where it might occur. Once, I told her, it happened on my way to work when I looked at the Bank of America building. I had no idea why. Neither my wife nor I had any connection to that building or the bank, so it didn't make sense. But grief doesn't always make sense.

I told her that I used to be a hospice volunteer. I suggested that maybe she join a hospice grief group. I chatted with her and listened to the pain of her loss. When she finally calmed down, we hugged, and she left the store.

I realized later that I wasn't there to check my AV equipment. I was there for something more important. I was somehow sent there to help a grieving woman.

Words Matter

I recall a minister who had been experiencing long bouts of depression because of the seeming lack of success in his parish. One day he went to visit a woman who was very ill. As he started to leave the room, the woman spoke to him: "You have been such an important person in my life. I want you to know that I have a great love for you." These kind words sailed straight into the minister's heart. He told me that he just couldn't believe in it but by the time he reached his office he could sense that something different was stirring within him. During the next several weeks the depression lifted, and he felt a tremendous rejuvenation in his life.

—Joyce Rupp, *Little Pieces of Light*

THE AWE FACTOR

KNOCK-ME-OVER AWE

It's a constant, continuous, spectacular world we live in and every day you see things that just knock you out, if you pay attention.

—Robert Irwin, artist

Ambassador of Light

A few years ago, I attended a workshop in which we created a vision board representing who we were or wanted to be. Mine had a big letter "A" in the center of it with gold foil in the triangle within the letter and rays of sunlight radiating out from behind it. My vision board showed not only bright rays of the sun but also had other images associated with light. There were lighted candles, hanging light bulbs, and strands of colorful Christmas tree lights. The board contained other aspects of my life too, but the most important items were the many sources of light.

After contemplating the images for a while, I realized that I was, as the board revealed, an "Ambassador of Light." Through both my keynote speeches and my books, I have touched many people's lives and helped them lighten up. "Ambassador of Light" was my perfect moniker.

Since working on the vision board and discovering what I believed to be my calling in life, I embrace it every day. But I have rarely, if ever, mentioned my self-designated title to others. Then, just a few days after creating the board, someone who I only know casually, thanked me for being in her life. She said she appreciated my joyful attitude and how it influenced her view of the world. She told me, and I quote, "You are an ambassador of light."

It was one of those "I-just-got-the-chills" moments. She had no idea how I had been referring to myself. Yet, there she was speaking the exact same words I was using to describe my "why." She got it. And I got to be awestruck.

Burn Survivors

Several years ago, I was asked to be the speaker and facilitator at an all-weekend retreat. I would be teaching burn survivors and their caregivers about therapeutic humor. The event consisted of my presenting the introductory session on Friday evening, then teaching all day and evening on Saturday, and finally concluding the retreat on Sunday morning. It was the most challenging program I had ever done in my entire speaking career, and, as it turned out, perhaps the most gratifying.

When I was first asked to do the retreat, I didn't know how I could possibly teach this group about therapeutic humor when they had been through such a horrible ordeal. First, I didn't know how I would react to their disfigurements. Second, I didn't know how I could sustain such a long period of time with them. Other thoughts ran through my head: Would I have enough material to fill the long weekend? Would what I was saying be relevant to them? After all, they had been through hell. I hadn't.

The truth was that all my fears were unfounded. They loved what I did. They jumped at any chance to laugh.

And once I got over the initial shock of seeing their deformities, all I could see was their radiant and beautiful spirits. They didn't know it, but they taught me more than I taught them.

They taught me about courage. They taught me about unconditional love as I watched their caregivers and loved ones attend to a burn survivor's every need.

They taught me that in spite of what they went through, they could laugh. In fact, they craved it.

There were several awe moments during the weekend but the one that amazed me the most happened during the last Sunday session. The attendees got in groups of about five people. I then instructed them to create a thirty-to-sixty-second TV-like commercial related to being a burn survivor. They could use anything in the room as a prop and/or any other device, such as a song, a poem, a parody, an acronym, a popular slogan, etc., to get their message across.

I gave the group about thirty minutes to complete the exercise and then asked which group would like to go first. That is when I was awed by what happened.

Two of the participants were a Black married couple. The husband had been severely burned in a work-related accident and his wife was his caregiver. Other than saying his name at the opening session on Friday night, he was silent the entire retreat. Every time a question came up in which the attendees were required to answer, his wife would be the one who replied.

So, I was genuinely amazed when the man was the first to raise his hand in order to perform the commercial the group had created. He got up and, using the group as backup singers, performed a rap song. I don't remember the exact words, and I wish I had a camera to record it, but I do recall that he began dancing around the room and singing in a loud joyful voice, "B-U-R-N, B-U-R-N, B-U-R-N..."

When he was done singing about what each of the letters stood for, the other attendees responded with loud cheers and applause. Those who could get up gave him a rousing standing ovation.

And all of this from someone who hadn't said a word all weekend.

The Human Body

Anannya Mondal, a medical student, posted this on Quora about our amazing bodies:

> When I was in first year, we had a subject called physiology. This subject basically deals with how the body works. And as I studied physiology, I was amazed. Awe is what I feel when I know that my heart pumps seventy times a minute every minute of my life.
>
> Awe is what I feel when I know that my kidneys filter 180 liters of blood every day.
>
> Awe is what I feel when I know my brain stores memories from when I was a child and it controls all my bodily functions.
>
> Awe is what I feel when I think of how my cerebellum and muscles coordinate to move my body.

The human body is a marvel of nature. It functions flawlessly. It is exquisite and unparalleled. We have created so many things but nothing as awesome as the human body.

Hindsight

As I get up in years, certain parts of my body start to malfunction. Joints don't move as easily as they did previously. My hearing is less sharp, eyesight less clear. I have to give up or cut back on certain foods which no longer digest as well as they did when I was younger. Things I've taken for granted and not even thought about now get my attention. All of it is making me more aware than I have ever been about how awesome our bodies are.

As in other aspects of our life, we don't appreciate the everyday awe of it until it is taken away from us.

—Allen Klein

The Three-by-Five-Inch Card

In spite of the fact that my books had sold more than 400,000 copies, the publishing company closed that division to cut costs. I got the rights back and proceeded to find a new publisher. Not finding one after searching for a year and a half, I gave up looking and put a three-by-five-inch card above my computer on which I wrote: *"The Perfect Publisher Will Find Me."*

Then one day, I went to a meeting of book publicists. I hadn't been to one of their meetings for years, but I wanted to hear the guest speaker they were having that day. At the event, the man next to me was chatting with two women behind him. I overheard them say that they were starting a new division of their publishing company and that they were looking for books that uplift, inspire, and bring joy to readers.

When I heard that, I immediately turned around and introduced myself. I told them about my out-of-print books and how perfect they were for their new division.

One of the women was the acquisition editor. She gave me her card and asked that I send her my books. When I saw their address, I knew that I found the perfect publisher. Their offices were five blocks from where I lived. I hand delivered my books the next day. They have published nine of my books since that chance encounter.

But that is only part of this amazing story. The truly awe-inspiring moment came shortly after I signed my first contract with them. They had a party to celebrate their new, larger headquarters. When I walked in the door, a woman greeted me and said that she owned the company and that she was pleased that I was one of their authors. She then said, "I know you." She told me that she now lived in London but that for sixteen years she lived across the street from me and saw me walk my dog every day.

I'm a firm believer in setting intentions to create what I want. By focusing on my *"The Perfect Publisher Will Find Me"* sign, I was drawing the energy I wanted toward me. And it worked.

What was so awesome for me was how it all unfolded and the fact that the publisher had been a neighbor of mine for so many years.

We can get a clue, perhaps, why things like this happen from what Sky Nelson-Isaacs writes about in his book *Living in Flow*. He reminds us, "When we align with circumstances, circumstances align with us."

The Penthouse

Tosha Silver is an author who writes about spiritual matters. In her book, *Outrageous Openness*, she shares a story about how the perfect living space came to her. She begins, "I'm a great believer in what some traditions would call *conjuring a miracle*, inviting Divine intercession on just about any topic, big or small... Over the years I've seen that calling in a miracle can open doors that linear rationality never could."

For three years Silver was bedridden because of an illness and lived in "a small, dark room with a mat on the floor and a hot plate." As she began to be well again, she longed for something better. But, not having worked for so long, her funds were low. She certainly didn't need anyone to tell her how outrageously high the rents were in San Francisco. Nevertheless, she was open to a miracle. "Jeez," she says, "I had just returned from the dead. I had nothing to lose."

One day while out for a walk, she saw a sign: *Penthouse for Rent*. An amiable-looking guy was standing nearby and asked Silver if she wanted to see it.

"Well, I can't imagine how I could ever afford such a place," she laughed, "but why *not*?"

They went upstairs where Silver found an amazing place—floor-to-ceiling views of the Golden Gate Bridge, vaulted skylights, hardwood floors.

"I don't even dare ask what this costs," she sighed.

The guy asked what she was currently paying. The penthouse was supposed to rent for a couple of thousand a month, but he offered it to her for only two hundred dollars more than her current rent.

He said, "I grew up in the Damascus streets and learned by the age of four to read someone's character on the *spot*... The minute you walked up I knew three things: I could trust you, you'd been through a disaster, and I want you to live here. You were perfect."

The Apartment

I was born and raised in New York City. For the past forty-plus-years or so, I've lived in San Francisco, but I visit my hometown about once a year.

Whenever I'd visit, I used to stay with my cousin who lived in Queens, but she passed away. After that I either rented an apartment from an acquaintance who has a time-share there, or from a friend who lives in Connecticut but has an apartment in Manhattan. One particular year, however, the first apartment wasn't available, and my friend had just sold his place. So, I had nowhere to stay.

Then, one evening, I accompanied my husband to a dinner that took place during his annual therapist's conference in San Francisco. During the cocktail hour, a woman from way across the room, who neither I nor my husband knew, walked over to us. She looked me straight in the eye and said, "You are so debonair. You are so cute. You are..." I did have on a jacket and nice tie, but nothing, I thought, to attract such glowing compliments. I kidded with her and said, "Lady, be careful. My husband is standing right next to me."

After we stopped laughing, I asked her where she was from. She said, "New York City."

"We will be going there in a few months," I said. "We usually have a place to stay but this time we don't. Do you know of any apartment we could rent for a week?"

She wanted to know what month and the dates we would be there. I told her it would be during the last week in May.

She said, and this is the incredible jaw-dropping part, "We will be in Italy that week. You can stay at our place." When I asked what she would charge us, she said "Nothing. We just like someone to be there when we are away."

We will be visiting New York City again next month. Of course, we will be staying at this great twenty-four-hour-doorman apartment on West End Avenue. And this will be the fifth time we have done so.

Each time we do, I am awed by how this all came about. After all,

- I wasn't a member of the organization hosting the event
- I was simply tagging along with my husband
- she was not standing near us at the cocktail party; she had to walk clear across the room to chat with us
- there were about fifty other people in the room; she could have gone over to any one of them; she didn't, she came over to us

- ❄ her apartment was in New York City; we needed an apartment there
- ❄ she would be in Europe the last week of May; we would be in Manhattan that same week

What are the chances of all of those things coming together? Some people might say it is a coincidence. I think it is bigger than that. As quantum physics is revealing, we are all energy tapping into the energy of our surroundings and the people around us.

Maybe we can't explain moments like this. Maybe we just need to be awed by them and leave it at that.

The Cup

> I once bought an old metal drinking cup... Years later, I was moving into my third place and pulled the cup out. The guy helping me move that I'd hired off the street looked at the cup and said, "I think this is from my high school. We got these cups at prom and I lost mine." I just gave it to him. He called me back after a few days He'd had it cleaned and it turned out to be his cup!
>
> **—Dandy McCoogan, on Quora.com**

The Hot Tub

In *Living in Flow*, author Sky Nelson-Isaacs describes an incident not too unlike my apartment experience.

He was at a retreat center with a group of people to design a mobile phone app over the course of a weekend.

After a long day, he headed to the hot tub only to find an "out of order" sign on it. On the way back to his room, he encountered a complete stranger who saw his plight and invited him to join the meeting of another group. "It's an unexpected and unusual offer," says Nelson-Isaacs, so he changed out of his bathing suit and headed to the social hall. At the end of the evening, he found himself talking to a man named Michael who was interested in Nelson-Isaacs work on flow and synchronicity. The man mentioned the possibility of him speaking to a professional association to which he belonged.

A month later, a colleague who happened to be on the same association board as Michael called. She and Michael talked about him and decided he would be the perfect speaker for their next month's meeting.

Several weeks later he did the talk, which proved to be an important event in his professional path. He met several influential people who would help him with various aspects of his work. "How was I to know that a broken hot tub would lead to these valuable developments in my career?" he says.

Moreover Nelson-Isaacs says, and this is why it qualifies as an awe moment for me, "I learned later that the hot tub had actually been fixed, but the "out of order" sign had been left in place by accident!"

WHEN-YOU-LEAST-EXPECT-IT AWE

Awe...sneaks up on us. It doesn't ask our permission to wow us; it just does. Awe can arise from a single glance, a sound, a gesture.

—Sharon Salzberg, *Real Love*

The Offering Basket

When I was growing up, every opportunity to save a penny or two was taken. I remember an incident at my Bar Mitzvah celebration. Not only did my aunt and my mother make every bit of food but they sat for hours adorning each toothpick with fringed, colored cellophane. Something they probably could have bought at the five-and-dime store for under fifty cents a box.

Part of my young years was during World War II when things were rationed, and lessons in frugality surrounded me. I was forced to belong to the "clean-plate club" and eat everything on my plate whether I liked it or not. "Think about all those starving children in Europe," my mother would tell me. I not only learned about not wasting food but also about never being frivolous with money. Pennies were saved to buy war bonds and dimes were saved for the March of Dimes to help fight polio.

Fast-forward twenty-five years. I'm married and making good money as a scenic designer at CBS-television. Although my marriage was a happy one, the remnants of growing up worrying about money put a wedge in our relationship. I worked hard to earn it, and my wife would happily spend it. It wasn't until after she died that I began to understand the lesson she taught me. I learned that life is short and that money is merely energy that needs to be spread around and enjoyed while we are still alive.

But my awe moment about money didn't come until many years later. The incident that totally turned my "gotta-save-it" thinking around was when I learned about tithing; giving 10 percent of your income to organizations that feed you spiritually. I wasn't sure about this tithing thing, but I made a tithing commitment to Unity San Francisco, the spiritual center I attended.

After several months of tithing, a distant relative died and left me a significant amount of money. The five-figure check was a total shock. What surprised me even more was what happened when I began to offer my tithe. As I sat in Sunday service, holding my several-thousand-dollar check in my hand, panic started to come over me. "How could I possibly give away all this money?" "What if I needed it in the future?" "Why give it away when I could use it for a trip to Europe, or buy a high-fashion suit, or eat at several fancy restaurants?"

The offering basket got closer and closer as I was getting more and more agitated. Then it was decision time. The basket was just a few feet away and being passed to me. Trembling, I dropped the check in it. Suddenly something happened that I never expected and will never forget. The panic dissipated, and a wave of euphoria came over me. I felt a sense of joy like I've never felt before. I was smiling and elated. I just gave away a bunch of money, but I felt like I won the lottery.

Later on, I thought about why I got such a reaction when I was previously having so many misgivings. I couldn't exactly explain the exaltation, but I did realize a number of things.

First, giving away the money did not make me any poorer. Sure, if you added up my assets before and after I put the check in the offering basket, it would show that I had less money. In reality, however, I was actually feeling much richer knowing that I had enough resources to help others.

Even more than that, the major revelation I got from this awe moment, was that clutching on to anything and withholding it (like money, love, talent, etc.), does not support an abundant life.

Stranger in the Corner

Shortly after my wife died, I became the director of the Life-Death Transitions Institute at the Holistic Life Institute in San Francisco. It was also a time when Norman Cousins was writing about how he used humor to help cure his debilitating illness. Since my wife had a great sense of humor, I was intrigued about the connection between humor and illness, and particularly about humor in end-of-life issues.

I enrolled in an independent master's degree program where I delved heavily into those subjects, although at the time there was hardly anything written about their connection. Part of the program involved giving a three-hour colloquium discussing what I had learned from my research.

Near the break, I spotted a woman in the corner of the room who looked exactly like my deceased wife. I hadn't noticed her up to that time but seeing her caused me to audibly gasp. I stopped momentarily then managed to continue with the program. I planned to speak to her at the break.

When that time came, I immediately headed in her direction only to be interrupted by someone tapping me on my shoulder to ask a question. When I turned around again to approach the woman, she was gone. And she never returned after the break.

I can't really say if that woman who looked like my wife was really there or if she was in my imagination. I have come to believe, however, that this awesome experience was a sign from my wife indicating that she supported what I was doing. She was encouraging me to keep telling a hurting world the importance of therapeutic humor.

FULL-CIRCLE AWE

You know, if you hang around this earth long enough you really see how things come full circle.

—Patti Davis, actress

The Mandino Connection

In addition to having authored such self-help books as *The Healing Power of Humor, You Can't Ruin My Day,* and *Embracing Life After Loss,* I am also the author of a number of inspirational and motivational quotation books. Those all began as a result of my contact with Og Mandino, author of *The Greatest Salesman in the World,* which has sold more than fifty million copies.

Mandino was speaking at a conference I was attending and announced that if anyone in the audience had an idea for a book, they should come up to the stage and get a label addressed to his publisher. Instead of taking months to respond, which was typical of busy publishers, they would reply within two weeks because of that specially marked label.

I had collected hundreds of quotations from my first book on therapeutic humor but only used a handful at the beginning of each chapter. I thought the lighthearted quotes I had amassed would make an interesting book. I submitted my idea. The publisher liked it and released the book in 1991.

The Mandino connection led to a series of other quotation books published in various formats by several other publishers. They were very successful, selling more than 400,000 copies. Of course, I was very pleased about their popularity, but over the years I had forgotten how it all started. That was until I got a letter from a teenager. Below is an excerpt of what she wrote:

> I know there are hundreds of other inspiring quote books in the world, yet it was your book that helped save my life.
>
> My dad passed away when I was eleven and just beginning to win over my own personal battle with depression. I had been searching through my over-flowing pile of books within a few weeks after my dad's death when I come across yours.
>
> I remember the birthday when my dad gave me the book and how I hadn't been too thrilled with the gift. But upon opening it and reading such touching words, I have been struck with an emotion so deep and powerful, I still don't know of any words to describe it—I only know it was then that I began to find myself. I had glimpsed my first twinkle of starlight in the dark, cloudy sky in the pages of your book. With each quote I read, a new star shone bright.
>
> Now my quote book is laid out in a special spot, right in front of the picture of my dad, next to a few keepsakes I keep to remind me of the time he was here with me.

I have a picture of my dad marking the page with the quote: *"I will love the light for it shows me the way. Yet I will endure the darkness for it shows me the stars."*

Upon reading the letter, I was both awed and floored; tears welled up in my eyes and chills ran down my spine. Things had come full circle. You see, the quotation was by Og Mandino.

A Word from the Pew

"In college," says Peter Albert, "I had the opportunity to study in Montreal, to revisit my Québec roots and the relatives I'd admired as a child. They were devout, and I knew they'd appreciate my attending Mass with them. But I couldn't abide the charade of going somewhere that preached eternal damnation for people whose sole sin was not being Catholic."

To ease his anxiety before visiting his religious relatives, Albert contacted a church near his home in California. This is what happened next:

> Father Chris surprised me. He was young, intellectual, and eager to be challenged. And I was defiant. I told him, "I can't support a religion that's founded on punishment!" Then he really surprised me. "I don't believe in Hell, myself," he admitted.
>
> "What do you mean?" I stammered. "You're a priest!"
>
> "I understand God differently," Father Chris explained. "He doesn't want people to suffer. If there's a Hell, it's here on earth, while we are living. But that can be our heaven, too."

I can't explain how satisfying it was for a nineteen-year-old to hear this from a priest. With awe and appreciation and some inspiring conversations, Father Chris administered my first Communion. He embraced me, telling me that *I* renewed *his* faith too.

Albert continues:

That was our last conversation. I enjoyed attending Mass with my Québec relatives. I got married at Mission San Luis Obispo to a non-Catholic. We moved to San Francisco, where I baptized our two children. I never pressured my family to attend Mass with me. My belief was personal.

Then, during the AIDS crisis, it was shaken. My parish church seemed to preach homophobic retribution. I found another church that supported gay Catholics. However, I misread the Mass schedule and showed up an hour early. As I sat idle, I noticed a bulletin in my pew announcing a memorial gathering next week—for Father Chris.

He had just died of AIDS.

At the memorial, his elderly parents were grief-stricken. "If it wasn't for Chris," I said as I took their hands, "I wouldn't be Catholic. I wouldn't have baptized my children. He made all the difference."

I could see my words mattered.

Twenty years before, his words had mattered to me. And miraculously, here we were.

Albert says that "If I'd missed that Mass, or if I got there on time and didn't fidget around looking for something to read to pass the time, I'd have never known Father Chris passed away. And I certainly wouldn't have been able to meet his parents."

Call it a series of coincidences, call it an awe moment, call it a twist of fate or the work of the hand of God, it doesn't really matter. What does matter was Albert's extraordinary experience and his being "doubly grateful to have been in that pew on that day, in that moment."

FAMILIAR-OBJECTS AWE

When you choose to see the glory that lies within even the obvious and mundane, then that fly on the window, or simple cloud in the sky, or hand in your hand, is as much an invitation to awe as the Grand Canyon or the pyramids.

—Alan Morinis, *Everyday Holiness*

More than seventy years ago, I went on a school field trip to the Hayden Planetarium in New York City where we saw a "Trip to the Moon" show. At the conclusion, each student received a small yellow card reserving a space for them on a future moon trip. I kept that card with me for years, just in case such a trip would ever become a reality. Of course, it did, but only for a very few.

Most of us will never get a chance to walk on the moon and have the awe experience that the astronauts did. Yet, every day, the commonplace has the power to awe us. As Jonah Paquette, PsyD, notes, "We don't have to climb to the summit of Mount Everest, or stand atop the Eiffel Tower, to reap the many benefits of awe. Instead, we can learn to notice the changing colors of the leaves, truly see the joy in a child's eyes, or allow ourselves to be uplifted by the kindness of a stranger."

The Refrigerator

I was listening to a radio show the other day in which three men, who had been in prison for at least five years, were about to be released. The reporter asked all of them the same question: "What are a few things you are looking forward to doing when you get out of prison?"

Most of them replied with what one might expect from someone who had been incarcerated to say—"spending time with my family," "going to a baseball game," "seeing my friends again." But one prisoner said something that took me by surprise. The thing he was looking forward to the most was, "to open the refrigerator."

How many times a day do we open the refrigerator without thinking about it? Yet here was a young man who was looking forward to this simple everyday act bringing him great joy.

After hearing him say that, I realized that there was deeper meaning in his answer. It revealed his restricted freedom and lack of control of his own life while being locked up. He couldn't get any food or drink whenever he wanted. His meals, and his choice of what he ate, were mandated by others. Even getting up and getting a glass of milk or a cold soda was denied.

Is it any wonder then that for this man even the thought of simply opening the refrigerator was awe-inspiring?

The Raisin

I've attended many personal growth workshops, weekend retreats, seminars, lectures, and keynote presentations over the course of my lifetime. I've done the est personal growth training consisting of several weekends where you could not leave the room for hours, even for a bathroom break. I've participated in ten-day silent meditation retreats where the only sound of another human voice was an occasional evening dharma talk by the facilitator. And I've been both a participant and an organizer at several death-and-dying retreats where many of the participants were either close to death themselves or closely connected to someone who was.

All of them were extremely powerful. Yet if I had to choose one moment from all of them that influenced my life the most, it would be the day I held a simple raisin in my hand. It was part of an exercise near the end of one retreat. A group of about thirty of us were taken to a hillside where we were seated and given a single raisin.

We were told not to eat it immediately but instead to simply look at it, to see its color and texture, to think of its history and how it began, to realize what it took to sustain it and the process to transform it from a grape into a raisin. Once we felt that we had explored the raisin long enough, we were then asked to put it in our mouth. We slowly examined it with our tongue, our teeth, and our taste buds, as we slowly, very slowly, chewed and finally swallowed it.

It was a simple process but, for me, a profound one. It opened my eyes to seeing what a special gift the raisin was, what a long and remarkable journey it was to get it to me, and how, in the entire world there was no other raisin that looked, or tasted, exactly like the one I had experienced.

Suddenly I discovered a world of wonder in a raisin. And in all the food I would be consuming from then on.

Bubbles

Bubbles have always filled me with wonder and awe. I've seen professional bubble blowers fill them with smoke, create multiple bubbles inside one another, and even make a spinning bubble carousel. But they need not be that elaborate to be awesome. Their glistening beauty attracts both adults and kids alike. And their short lives make them even more special.

I once had a very simple bubble device that consisted of nothing more than a circle of cotton fringe attached to some doweling. When I dipped it into a basin of soapy liquid and slowly moved the wand around, it made super gigantic bubbles. What was so amazing was that, because of their size, the bubbles no longer kept their perfectly round shape. Instead some were long, some fat, and some a changing, undulating shape as they floated through the air.

In their intrinsic attractive and awesome nature, bubbles are like people. They are beautiful to look at and shimmer with wonderful and varied colors. They come in a multitude of sizes and shapes. Like life, they are here one moment and gone the next.

It is why I want everyone who attends my celebration of life after I am gone to be given a container to make bubbles and remember me by releasing them in the air.

FINAL AWE

I often wondered what it was about my looming death that could sometimes make me feel more in awe of being alive than I had before I became sick—in addition to being in what felt like a strange awe of death that has not left me to this day.

—Paul Pearsall, *AWE: The Delights and Dangers of Our Eleventh Emotion*

When I was a hospice volunteer, there was something both peaceful and frightening about being with someone who had just died. Peaceful as when all previous pain passed away; suddenly it seemed like something left their body, some burden that they no longer had to endure. Frightening because one moment they were there, and the next gone. In a sense, both of these made for an awe-filled moment.

There was also something of awe in knowing that death, especially of the elderly, forms a full circle of life. When we are born, we need to be dressed, fed, bathed, diapered, and made comfortable, among other things. When we are in the dying process, we too often need assistance with our feeding, dressing, bathing, bowel care, comfort, and more.

When I think about awe's relationship to death, I also see a connection to a higher power or something outside of ourselves. I particularly noticed this as a hospice volunteer. A couple of my patients, who were less than twenty-four hours from dying, exclaimed such things as, "I want to go up" or more symbolically, "Get me up. I want to go around the block."

On another level too, when we are born our spirit, or whatever you wish to call it, enters this world. We really don't know where that spirit comes from. Nor do we know where it goes when we die. In between, we live in the mystery of it all.

What we do know is that the essence of who we are while on earth remains. Perhaps that is our spirit. Perhaps it doesn't go anywhere but remains to provide comfort for those left behind.

The Last Breath

My longtime friend Liam Cunningham thinks of awe as being an "ah-ha" moment. One of those moments happened to him when he was in the hospital with his brother Patrick, who was dying from ALS disease. Liam noticed that his brother's breathing kept changing. Then suddenly, it stopped.

"I was amazed at the distinction between life and death," my friend observed. "One moment we are breathing and the next we are not. One moment my brother is a living human being and the next he was a corpse."

Liam experienced what a lot of people usually don't—being with someone when they die, at the very moment they stop breathing—the very moment of death.

Liam also observed how we often don't honor that moment. When his brother died both Patrick's wife and mother-in-law were in the hospital room. Instead of sitting for a while with her just-deceased husband, and perhaps allowing some time for loved ones to at least say their goodbyes, she immediately wanted to call the undertaker. Liam comments, "We are so in a hurry to go on to the next thing—the funeral arrangements and all that busyness."

Because of my experience as a hospice volunteer, I know how special it can be to be around the dying. In addition, I also used to manage Stephen Levine's death-and-dying workshops and retreats. Levine was the author of several books on the subject, including my favorite, *Who Dies*. He was a great teacher for thousands of people, including myself.

Liam's contemplation about the moment of death reminded me of an unanswerable, but profound, question Levine asked his attendees: "Are you going to die on an in breath or an out breath?"

The Power to Awe

But death, too, had the power to awe, she knew this now—that a human being could be alive for years and years, thinking and breathing and eating, full of a million worries and feelings and thoughts, taking up space in the world, and then, in an instant, become absent, invisible.

—**Jhumpa Lahiri,** *Unaccustomed Earth*

What's in a Name?

When I'm writing a book, at some point I scour the internet to see what other information is out there related to my topic. I found several videos related to awe. One was by author Francis Chan on "The Awe Factor of God." Since I found his information interesting, I explored some of his other videos. Several of them said they were recommended to him by Martin Schwartz. That is when my oh-my-God moment of awe arose.

I had a distant relative named Martin Schwartz. He was a good friend who I would see often when I lived in New York City. He is also the one who left me a large amount of money that I write about earlier in this book. He died about ten years ago.

I know Martin Schwartz is a pretty common name, but the fact that I hadn't seen his name for years, and that it was so closely connected to a discussion about the universe's energy, blew me away. I was also blown away by what came next.

Curious what else I might discover, I searched the internet for Martin Schwartz, New York City. What came up was a dentist with the same name. And, amazingly, his office was a mere two blocks from where my friend had lived.

A coincidence perhaps. But for me these are signs to remind us to keep the memory of those we have lost alive.

PART THREE

AWE-WAKENING PRESCRIPTIONS

Awe is there to be had in any moment... We all have those moments, often in nature, often in encounter with another soul, when we are visited by a sense of depth and levels of reality that we do not ordinarily perceive. To open ourselves to these moments without reservations...makes it possible to gain more of the gift these moments hold for us.

—Alan Morinis, *Everyday Holiness*

In his TEDx presentation, philosopher Jack Bowen says that if you believe "that everything, from the seemingly mundane to the grandiose, is filled with an experience of awe...everyone with whom you interact, everything you do, and everything you see...then you cannot *not* experience... happiness, gratitude, compassion, and mindfulness."

This last section of the book will provide you with tools, tips, and techniques to help you achieve that "experience of awe." Some you may find useful, and some perhaps not. Take what fits and leave the rest behind. If you receive just a few ideas of how to get more awe in your life, then I have done my job.

STOP.

LOOK.

LISTEN.

SLOW DOWN

I began to think that there was something awesome about my timing. How was it that, at the exact moment of my stopping, such incredible things were happening? It took me longer than I am prepared to admit to realize that such things were always happening. It was only that I was finally paying attention.

—Mark Epstein, *Going to Pieces without Falling Apart*

While I am writing this, we are in the midst of the coronavirus pandemic in which many of us are sheltering in place. One would think that there would be little to appreciate about these confining circumstances, yet one man I heard on the radio this morning said that he was very grateful. Instead of rushing through his chores, as he usually does, he has slowed down and really appreciates doing them. He mentioned things like doing the dishes, feeling the warmth of the water, interacting with the soapsuds, and getting comfort knowing they were clean.

In *Music of Silence*, author David Steindl-Rast shares the following story about slowing down:

> In the 1995 film *Smoke*, Auggie Wren manages a cigar store on the corner of Third Street and Seventh Avenue in Brooklyn. Every morning at exactly eight o'clock, no matter what the weather, he takes a picture of the store from across the street. He has four thousand consecutive daily photographs of his corner all labeled

by date and mounted in albums. He calls this project his "life's work."

One day Auggie shows the photos to Paul, a blocked writer who is mourning the death of his wife, a victim of random street violence. Paul doesn't know what to say about the photos; he admits he has never seen anything like them. Flipping page after page of the albums, he observes with some amazement, "They're all the same." Auggie watches him, then replies: "You'll never get it if you don't slow down, my friend."

OPEN THE DOOR TO AWE

Find some object in your environment that pleases you.

For the next three days, take a picture of it with your phone.

Make sure that it is from the same spot each time.

Then, after the third day, compare the photos. What do you notice that's different?

Take the Time

I do not need to be at the seashore or on a mountaintop to enjoy the cosmic dance. I only need to be awake and alert, to let go of my busyness and my self-absorption, in order to discover mystery and wonder.

—Joyce Rupp, *The Cosmic Dance*

Many of us get so busy that we neglect to stop for a moment and take the time to enjoy our surroundings. Our days rush by without us contemplating what they entailed. Instead of relishing the essence of the day before it is totally over, we bury ourselves in our computers or the late-night news. Is it no wonder then that our awe moments are ignored because we are too busy to even recognize them?

In the book *Repacking Your Bags* by Richard J. Leider and David A. Shapiro, there is a wonderful story about taking time to observe the world around us. While not necessarily an awe moment, it does illustrate the amusing things that can happen when we simply stop and take some time.

> I was sitting in the café, nursing a glass of Bordeaux, affecting a pose of resigned world weariness. I've observed the passersby outside on the street going through the pointless motions of human life, and my heart was filled with deep existential despair. A small dog appeared, and while I watched, deposited a large turd on the sidewalk just in front of the café entrance. It seemed to me to be the perfect metaphor for the filth and aggregation of everyday existence.

> I ordered another glass of wine and resolved to sit and watch until someone stepped into the mess, feeling that this would sum up perfectly how we move through our days—blithely wandering along until, all of a sudden, and for no reason at all, we are soiled with foul and noxious excrement.

The show turned out to be quite amusing—and exciting as hell. Person after person would almost step into it, but at the last second, either notice and move aside, or just miss it. It was like watching a daredevil high-wire act at the circus. I started to have a great time. I was smiling, laughing out loud.

We not only need to take time to allow awe to enter our life, but we must make room for it as well. As Karen Scalf Linamen says in her light-heartedly titled book, *Just Hand Over the Chocolate and No One Will Get Hurt,* "If our emotional files are too full, our Daytimers are crammed, and our brains are blinking O V E R L O A D! in neon letters and threatening to crash the system at any moment, what can we do about it? What is the answer that will save us from ourselves?"

"I have one word of advice," she says, "*Delete.*"

OPEN THE DOOR TO AWE

The things you see while driving are much different than the things you would have seen if you had walked or biked. The next time you have a chance to walk somewhere that you would otherwise take some wheeled transportation, do it.

As you do, stop and make note of things that capture your attention.

Be Present

Too often the reason we do miss the wonder of the now is that we are preoccupied with the past or the future.

—Robert J. Wicks, *Snow Falling on Snow*

In the movie *Postcards from the Edge*, one of the characters sends a card home from vacation that reads, "Having a wonderful time. Wish I were here." While that is an amusing line, it also has a lot of truth to it.

Often, we are so obsessed with thinking about the past or what might happen in the future that we miss what is happening in the present. Again, is it any wonder then that awe moments pass us by?

The spiritual teacher Ram Dass passed away recently so there were a number of tributes to him. In one of the videos, it showed him, not very long before his death, eating dinner with a friend. During the main course, the friend mentioned the dessert he had brought, which Ram Dass really liked. "No," said Ram Dass, indicating that the friend needed to focus on the food in front of them, not on what was to come.

OPEN THE DOOR TO AWE

One way to begin to have a greater awareness of the magic in your life is, as Nicki Verploegen Vandergrift suggests in *Organic Spirituality*, to "take some time to review the day for moments of awe and wonder."

She suggests: "Note how you receive them. If you missed them, or dismissed them, how could you cultivate greater receptivity the next time? Do this at least once or twice a day (noon and evening). It can help heighten awareness, opening our eyes to little things that begin to present themselves for greater appreciation."

SET YOUR ANTENNA

What you pay attention to grows.

—Deepak Chopra, spiritual teacher

When I'm writing a book on a certain subject, suddenly my antenna, my energy field, starts to attract information, stories, and things people say about that subject. It seems to fall into my lap just at the time I need it, but it only seems that way. In reality, it is coming my way because my antenna is up. I am more open and aware of receiving that information. It's almost like an old TV antenna; turn it in one direction and you get the channels you want. Turn it in another and you don't.

Sometimes we don't see awe-inspiring things even when they are right in front of us. In his book *Awe: Why It Matters for Everything We Think, Say, and Do*, author Paul David Tripp has an amusing story about this:

> I remember taking my youngest son to one of the national art galleries in Washington, DC. As we made our approach, I was so excited about what we were going to see. He was decidedly unexcited. But I just knew that, once we were inside, he would have his mind blown and would thank me for what I had done for him that day. As it turned out, his mind wasn't blown; he wasn't even activated. I saw things of such stunning beauty that brought me to the edge of tears. He yawned, moaned, and complained his way through

gallery after gallery. With every new gallery, I was enthralled, but each time we walked into a new art space, he begged me to leave. He was surrounded by glory but saw none of this. He stood in the middle of wonders but was bored out of his mind.

Museums and galleries are potential places for awe because their works of art can take us out of the ordinary. They open our eyes to seeing in new ways. Take, for example, Andy Warhol's interpretation of a Campbell's soup can or Georgia O'Keeffe showing us the inside of a flower.

OPEN THE DOOR TO AWE

When was the last time you were at an art museum? Maybe it is time you visited one again. (These days, you can even do that on the internet, but seeing a piece of art in person is the only way to truly experience its size, colors, and textures.)

Once at the museum, find a painting that calls out to you and stay with it for a while.

What is it saying to you?

What makes it special?

Does it get you to see its subject matter in a new way?

Pay Attention

*The moment one gives close attention to anything,
even a blade of grass, it becomes a mysterious,
awesome, indescribably magnificent world in itself.*

—Henry Miller, author

Technology is one of the biggest challenges these days, as well as one of the biggest enablers, for seeing the awe that surrounds us. Our computers abound with videos of nature scenes and incredible pets doing amazing things which could inspire ongoing awe. But technology is also a major awe-distracter.

Cell phones, podcasts, Facebook, Twitter, LinkedIn, email, instant messaging, iTunes, Instagram, and Snapchat all kidnap us away from the world around us. As a result, we lose those things that might awe us. Instead of being overwhelmed by sunrises, sunsets, and shooting stars, we are now distracted by cyberspace, supercomputers, and virtual reality.

Of course, the latter can fill us with awe too but in a different way. I suspect they don't nurture our soul. If we want to add more awe to our life that does nurture us, we need to pay less attention to the mechanical and more to the miraculous.

Distractions

I was struck by the fact that I hadn't been awed in a while. Did that mean awesome things had disappeared from my life? No. What it did mean was that I'd gotten too caught up in distractions and mind mucking to recognize anything as awe-inspiring... I hadn't been paying attention to the beauty around me.

—Sue Patton Thoele, *The Mindful Woman*

OPEN THE DOOR TO AWE

One of the ways you can increase your attention to the things around you is to be more mindful of whatever you are doing. Try this while eating a meal: First observe what is on your plate—the colors, textures, and aromas of the foods. Then slowly pick up the fork and bring a bite of food to your mouth. Like the raisin story earlier in the book, carefully chew the food before you swallow it, again noticing the textures and taste. Do this meditative eating until you finish the meal.

Once you have become familiar with this mindful technique, use it to sharpen your attention skills elsewhere.

BE MINDFUL OF MIRACLES

Are you taking notice of, and celebrating the miracles in your life? Or did you miss them because you were ruminating on the fact that you only received eleven likes on your last Instagram post?

—Randy Gage, from his blog *Success and Prosperity*

In the Broadway musical *Flower Drum Song*, there is a Rogers and Hammerstein song which reminds us that "a hundred million miracles" are happening every day. According to the lyrics, they include such things as changing weather, rivers flowing, flowers blooming, stars glistening, and a child's first steps. As the song reminds us, every minute so many wondrous things are going on. If we take them for granted, we miss the miracles around us.

Your Life Is a Miracle

Randy Gage is a colleague of mine whose wise words I've quoted above. In one of his blogs, Gage wrote about how we often focus on what we have lost instead of the miraculous nature of the life we have. This was brought front and center not too long ago for Gage, who loves baseball, when he injured himself in a game and could not play for the rest of the season. He started to feel sorry for himself until he realized, in his words, "My life is a f**king miracle."

Gage invites all of us to consider the miracles in our life. "Do you realize how blessed you are to be alive today—in the greatest time to be alive in human history? The fact that you have a cell phone or laptop to read this blog on. The fact that you have Wi-Fi or can have a coffee in a Starbucks and use theirs. You get the chance to experience at least a dozen miracles every day of your life. If you're looking for them."

One of the most important points Gage makes is contained in his last five words: "If you're looking for them." The choice is always yours. You can see the muck or the miracle in anything. And as he reminds us, that doesn't mean that life is:

> all peaches, gumdrops, and unicorns... You face challenges, setbacks, and obstacles too. *But remember something...*

Your life is a...miracle.

- If your car needs repair, it sucks. But isn't it a blessing to own a car?
- Maybe you're angry at your spouse right this minute. But aren't you grateful you have one to be angry with?
- Maybe you've also got an injury or disability right now. But how many wonderful things has your body allowed you to experience?
- You've probably lost people you love. But are their memories a blessing for you?

Perhaps the greatest miracle of all is being alive. And the greatest tragedy of all is how little we honor that miracle.

What Are the Chances?

There is 1 chance in 140 trillion that the earth should exist. There is 1 chance in 795 billion that life should have evolved on earth. There is 1 chance in 89 billion that life should have evolved into mankind. There is 1 chance in 12 billion that mankind should have created the alphabet and thus civilization. There is 1 chance in 6 billion that your parents should ever have met and got together. There is 1 chance in 90 million that you should have been the lucky sperm that fertilized your mother's egg...

Your very coming into being is miraculous.

—Ben Carey, *This Book Will Change Your Life*

Your Meal Is a Miracle

The next time you sit down to eat, don't immediately pick up your fork. Take a few minutes to look at the food and think about what it took to get each part of the meal to the table.

Consider that somebody had to prepare the meal. Maybe they also cut, peeled, chopped, and seasoned it. They went to the market to purchase what you are about to chow down. Then there is the person at the checkout stand, the person who shelved what was bought, and before that the delivery person who brought the items to the market. Someone also had to either pick the produce, slaughter the animal, or catch the fish. To begin the entire process, someone had to plant and water the seeds or feed and raise the animal.

Getting your food is a lengthy and slow process that, depending on what you are eating, might have taken months or even years to get to your plate. Most of the time we rarely think about the incredible journey. But if we stop for a moment to ponder the incredible trip, it is truly a miraculous one.

Food, Glorious Food

Wild black mushrooms shimmer in a glossy red sweet-and-sour sauce, leafy greens are bright and fresh and warmed with ginger. Spicy bean curd is flecked with fiery red peppers. Tiny slivers of carrots, fresh-sliced bamboo shoots, and deep-fried gluten puffs float in golden sesame sauce.

I stare at the food in awe, my mind blank.

—Anne Scott, *Serving Fire*

OPEN THE DOOR TO AWE

Every evening, write down a couple of small or large miracles that you noticed that day.

THE AWE FACTOR

BE MINDFUL OF MYSTERY

When you are tuned into the subtle experiences and insights and events and threads of your life, you are in touch with the energy that is guiding you... We are never separated from it—and that is where our awesome comes from. We don't have to know how it works; we can simply trust that it does.

—Polly Campbell, *How to Live an Awesome Life*

Because awe is hard to define, and the experience of it hard to describe, there is something inherently mysterious about it. We question how some magical incident could have happened.

Those places of mystery can move us in ways in which we never imagined. They bring us to our core—to our spiritual center. As author Nicki Verploegen Vandergrift points out in *Organic Spirituality*, "They can rekindle our natural ability to move into awe and cultivate wonder in everyday life."

Embrace the Mystery

This world is a relentless mystery, and so is our existence. Where did we come from? Why are we here? What happens after we die? If we are not comfortable with these mysteries, spending time in quiet solitude can be something we loathe and try to avoid at all costs. When faced with it, we immediately turn on the television, text a friend, or invite someone over for drinks. But when we embrace these mysteries and allow them to infuse us with a sense of adventure and awe, quiet solitude can be something we revel in and happily anticipate.

—**Tess Whitehurst,** *The Art of Bliss*

Many years ago, I took the est (Erhard Seminars Training) training. One of the things I remember learning from those weekends is that *not knowing* is one of the highest forms of knowledge and that "understanding is the booby prize." When we are certain of something, and only see something one way, we have taken away the possibility of it being any other way; we have taken the mystery out of it. Not knowing opens all sorts of doors to the way things might be and the mystery of the unknown.

The genius of Albert Einstein was developed because of his inquisitive nature toward the mystery of things. As a child, he was a slow learner and slow to speak. He later explained that it was actually an advantage. It allowed him "to observe with wonder" everyday things that others took for granted. His investigation of the commonplace at an early age led him to do the same with the cosmos in later years.

Einstein reminds us that "the most beautiful thing we can experience is the mysterious. It is the source of all true art and science. He to whom this emotion is a stranger, who can no longer pause to wonder and stand rapt in awe, is as good as dead: his eyes are closed."

OPEN THE DOOR TO AWE

In fictitious murder mysteries, there is usually a conclusive ending. The murder is solved, the culprit caught. In life, things are different. Mysteries persist or take long times to be explained.

Identify one unsolved mystery in your life. List some ways that it enriches your life.

MANIFESTING AWE

If it were possible to summarize all mystical teaching in a single sentence, this one would come close: Make your state of mind more important than what you are doing.

—Hugh Prather, *The Little Book of Letting Go*

In my TEDx talk on the power of intention, I discuss several ways of manifesting what you desire. Some of those ideas could also apply to allowing more awe into your life.

Step One: Set Your Intention

Without intention, you may not get what you are seeking.

Imagine, for example, you are going on vacation. The car is packed, and you are ready to head out. You can't just get in your car, turn on the ignition, and hope to get to your destination. You have to know what that is and how to get there.

Manifesting awe is not much different. You have to set your intention on it, or you may not see it even as it surrounds you. As author Carlos Castaneda reminds us, "In the universe there is an immeasurable, indescribable force which shamans call intent, and absolutely everything that exists in the entire cosmos is attached to intent."

Step Two: Commit

Once you commit to things in your life, things line up in support. As the German writer Goethe tells us, "At the moment of commitment the entire universe conspires to assist you."

Over and over in my life, I have found that if I make a commitment to something, it gets accomplished. It can be as basic as committing to write a book by a certain date, or as fanciful as wanting to march in the Macy's Thanksgiving Day parade and using these manifesting techniques to make it happen. (I was in the 2013 parade. Did you see me there?)

Step Three: Make a Choice

In his book about awe, neuropsychologist Paul Pearsall reminds us that every day we have a choice to stop and smell the roses or not. "Every morning of our lives, we're given the chance to see the world anew," he says. "How we choose to use this daily physiological fresh start sets our course for 'just another day' or for one full of awe. Whether we languish or flourish is up to us and how easily awed we choose to be."

The bottom line then lies in the choices we make. We can choose to see awe in our daily encounters or not, either way our life goes on. But I contend that if we choose to find awe, particularly in the mundane, our life will be richer, and as researchers are finding, healthier too.

I Choose Awe

Today, I choose not to take my life for granted...

I am thankful for my life. This moment is a blessing. Each breath a gift. That I've been able to take so much for granted is a gift, too. But it's not how I want to live—not when gratitude is an option, not when wonder and awe are choices.

I choose gratitude. I choose wonder. I choose awe. I choose everything that suggests I'm opening myself to the miraculous reality of simply being alive for one moment more.

—Scott Stabile, March 5, 2016 blog post

OPEN THE DOOR TO AWE

What if you lived each day with the expectation of having at least one awe moment that day?

Affirming Awe

It's easier to ride the horse in the direction he's going.

—Werner Erhard, founder of the est training

Our thoughts and words are powerful tools to help us focus on what we want in our life and to draw them to us. That is why affirmations are an important aid to manifesting awe. They confirm and declare what we are seeking.

When I asked people to share an awe-inspiring story with me, some responded that they have never been awed. It was hard for me to comprehend but it became more believable when I realized that they may have blocked, not acknowledged, or refused to affirm such events happening in their life.

If you are one of those people, take heart. Awe moments are available to everyone. But you may need a little help in drawing them to you. One of the ways to do that is to affirm that they are already here.

OPEN THE DOOR TO AWE

Repeat these affirmations numerous times a day, or make up your own:

"My life is filled with awe."

"I notice and celebrate the awe that surrounds me."

"Every day I am awed by the wonders in the world."

STOP.
LOOK.
LISTEN.

LOOK AROUND

To experience wonder, you have to notice what's going on around you, and most of the time our lives are going by in a blur. We need to cultivate a new attitude toward time if we are to open ourselves again to wonder and heart-piercing surprise.

—Alan Jones and John O'Neil, *Seasons of Grace*

There are two myths about awe that can be dispelled says professor Dacher Keltner. The first is that awe is rare. He and his team surveyed people in thirty countries. A majority of those reported a feeling of awe two-and-a-half times a day.

The second myth about awe that can be dismissed is that we need to go somewhere special to find it. Keltner says, "It is everywhere around us. Awe is part of our everyday life that we really need to return to." Keltner and his team gathered 2,600 narratives from around the world about what brought people awe. Those who responded reported finding awe everywhere—from something wonderful their dad did, to the magic of a working can opener.

Awe need not be the sighting of a double rainbow after a summer rainstorm. It can be small everyday moments that bring magic and wonder into our lives too. In her book *The Cosmic Dance*, author and spiritual teacher Joyce Rupp writes about those times:

Maybe I am sitting in the park and I see a pair of robins perched on a thin mulberry branch, or walking down a city street and a wild gust of wind sweeps by my face. Perhaps I stand still for a bit by a clump of trees, breathing in the freshness of the pines. I might be hurrying through a store and get caught up with the vulnerability of an elderly couple helping each other navigate through the crowds. It might be the simple gesture of sipping a cup of freshly brewed coffee or brushing rain off my coat. Each of these moments invites me into an awareness of the unspoken dance of energy connecting me to what I am experiencing. I sense for a moment that there is a hidden bond between myself and what is around me.

As Keltner's research found, awe is everywhere. We just need to look around to see it.

Two Birds

The other day, I had just stepped out of my lecture hall. My fellow classmates and I streamed out of the building, onto the city sidewalk, walking to the next class/coffee/conversation.

I was waiting for the light to turn, so that I could cross the street, when I heard a sweet, familiar chirping. I looked up, and there was a bird, with a rich, red color at the beak and the end of its wings. It was singing, chirping happily in a winter bare tree. I had never seen a female cardinal before, but I knew it must be one...

Moments later, I caught sight of the male cardinal, chirping back at her, a few trees away. I felt a peculiar sense of awe, and raw joy. Two birds singing sweetly to each other as they sat in leafless trees, in the midst of cold gray sidewalks and buildings and people walking mindlessly underneath them.

Vibrant, simple beauty.

—Ellie Alexandria, on Quora.com

OPEN THE DOOR TO AWE

Look around. Where might awe be hiding?

LOOK CLOSER

The question is not what you look at, but what you see.

—Henry Thoreau, journal entry August 5, 1851

One Ant

"A prisoner lived in solitary confinement for years. He saw and spoke to no one and his meals were served through an opening in the wall." Thus writes Anthony de Mello in *Taking Flight.*

One day an ant came into his cell. The man contemplated it in fascination as it crawled around the room. He held it in the palm of his hand the better to observe it, gave it a grain or two, and kept it under his tin cup at night.

One day it suddenly struck him that it had taken him ten long years of solitary confinement to open his eyes to the loveliness of an ant.

Two Ants

In her book *How to Live an Awesome Life*, author Polly Campbell writes about the time she spent an hour watching two ants move a dead bee, which was probably a hundred times their size, a half a block. Campbell had plenty of other things to do that day. Still, she was transfixed and awed by nature's event happening like some miniature theatrical performance just for her.

Campbell notes that we've got to "slow down long enough to look at the cracks in the sidewalk, to see the cracks in our lives and find the amazing there too. This isn't something you wait for; it's something you explore and uncover and discover both within yourself and outside."

"Too often," she writes, "we overlook the ants. We judge them and walk over them, deeming them irrelevant to our lives, and we miss the moment and the awe that permeates everything."

OPEN THE DOOR TO AWE

Next time you see an ant, or something else seemingly insignificant, walking on the ground or your windowsill, stop for a while and notice its distinct features, how it moves and where is it going.

Hunting for Awe

I recently participated in a twenty-one-day online Wonder-hunt class given by Kim Kotecki, cofounder of Escape Adulthood. The purpose of the class was to help participants find more wonder in their lives by intentionally looking for it. Each day our assignment was to take a photo of a particular item. Yesterday was especially amazing for me. The challenge was to "find and photograph a heart in nature."

I posted the required photo and wrote: "I recently planted some morning glory seeds to grow up and around my front iron gate. It wasn't until yesterday that I noticed the leaves were all heart shaped. Then today, you asked for photos of hearts in nature. Life truly provides many connections." Kim commented, "Allen, WOW...that's pretty remarkable. Many would say 'a God wink.' "

The Wonder-hunt process got me to look closer at both the things around me and my life. It made me realize that I often don't see the wonder in things because I'm rushing through my day. I had been going in and out of my house for weeks not noticing that the morning glory leaves were heart shaped.

BE CURIOUS

Look up at the stars and not down at your feet. Try to make sense of what you see and wonder about what makes the universe exist. Be curious.

—Stephen Hawking, physicist

A Child's Curiosity

Several years ago, as I lunched at a restaurant that had an outdoor eating area, I witnessed firsthand a child's unashamed response to the world around him. It was perfect because I had Josh, my golden retriever, with me. I tied Josh up to a bench on the other side of a low, potted-hedge barrier that separated the diners from the street. Josh was content because he could see me, and I could eat my lunch in peace because I could see him.

As I was eating, a mother strolled by with her two-year-old son. The child was delighted to be able to play with the dog. Josh loved the attention and I, along with the child's mother, delighted in the scene. There were several wonderful moments but the most magical was watching the child's fascination with Josh's elusive plume-like tail.

The young boy would try to grab the wagging tail. Of course, that was impossible, but it didn't matter; it made it more fun for the youngster. Moreover, the movement of the tail created a breeze that delighted the child as much as his trying to catch it. At one point, in fact, the child moved his face as close as he could to the tail to get both the breeze and the tickling sensation as well. After about five minutes of this, something else caught the boy's attention and he moved on. But the experience left me in awe to see a child's sense of wonder and curiosity as he found magic in such a simple thing as a dog's tail.

Adapted from *Secrets Kids Know...*
That Adults Oughta Learn by Allen Klein

New Eyes

Seeing with new eyes is a gift children offer to us. I think of how many times a child has made me stop and look at an insect, a flower, a bird. I cherish the times a child has helped me focus on the wonder in the world around me.

—**Richard Broderick,** *Leather Tramp Journal*

A child's world is fresh and new and beautiful, full of wonder and excitement. It is our misfortune that for most of us that clear-eyed vision, that true instinct for what is beautiful and awe-inspiring, is dimmed and even lost before we reach adulthood.

—**Rachel Carson,** *The Sense of Wonder*

You have to see the world through the kaleidoscope eyes of a child. As if there is awe in everything.

—**André Leon Talley, fashion journalist**

When you are around children what wonderment rubs off on you?

How does seeing the world through the eyes of a child change what you see?

Recall one or two awe experiences you may have had as a child. Can you share them with your children or grandchildren?

Magic in Meandering

Curiosity may have killed the cat, but don't be afraid of it. It can help you get more awe in your life.

One internet blog related to curiosity is *Noodling Around SF*. The premise is to wonder around the nooks and crannies of where you live. One of the posts focusing on San Francisco presents beautiful photos along with short commentary on the places visited by blogger Sheila McElroy.

One posting, "Treasure About Town," involves seeking out three specific categories of items that might be discovered on an outing. In this case, it was images of etched words, embedded objects, and stenciled images. The blogger notes, "They can be found all over the city, if you just scan the sidewalk as you go instead of staring at the phone screen."

The blog shows photos of words both chiseled and written in cement, patterns of stones and objects embedded in the ground as well as images stenciled on the sidewalk. Of the inscribed messages, the blogger says, "Personally, I like finding intentions and humor scratched in the sidewalk. It's like having a note passed to me in class. A shared secret."

Of the embedded objects, she notes that they "sometimes require that I stop and bend down to see the detail. I like the intimacy of self and object while in the midst of a busy city. I guess it's my urban equivalent of stopping to smell the roses."

In order to train yourself to stop and be more open to awe, perhaps you, like the blogger, might want to be more curious about your surroundings as you make your daily rounds this week.

OPEN THE DOOR TO AWE

One of the things I like best about foreign travel is going to a city I have never been to before and just roaming the streets. I have no destination other than to people watch, window-shop, and wonder at the architecture. There is indeed magic in not knowing what you will discover. Try it the next time you travel, or even in your own city.

THE AWE FACTOR

FLOWER POWER

There are always flowers for those who want to see them.

—Henri Matisse, artist

Flower gardens are truly amazing, for their color, their shapes, and for their aromas. If you are seeking more awe in your life, do as author Alan Epstein suggests, "Spend time in a flower garden." In his book, *How to Have More Love in Your Life*, he writes:

> Stay there as long as you wish, but make sure your visit is long enough to take in the various charms that the world of blossoms and petals provide. You can sit in a chair or on the grass, lie down looking up at the flowers from below, or walk around...

> If the day is warm and sunny, savor the rays and imagine how the flowers must feel at this very moment. Look closely at the variety of blooms, at the different shapes and colors, at the way the individual blossoms grow out of their leafy sheaths. Now use your sense of smell to take in the stunning array of fragrance, all of which can be divinely overpowering.

Epstein takes the garden interaction one step further and perhaps closer to an awe experience. He writes, "Now see if you can transcend your individual senses and feel the presence of the garden inside you. Try to become just another flower, at home in the garden."

Power of a Peony

One of the qualities of awe is its connection to vastness. We might associate that with some grand vista of open space, but it doesn't necessarily have to be that. In their book *Sacred World,* authors Jeremy and Karen Hayward discuss experiencing that vastness when exploring a flower close-up:

> When you look at a peony, you first see the whole flower, its color and shape. As you keep looking, you see the petals and veins and stamens and pistils. When you look more closely still, you see the segments and shading in the petals, until you begin to feel you could go deeper and deeper into those details. Then you can begin to feel a sense of vastness, a connection to vast space and to all other things.

A Single Rose

"I vividly remember a time when I completely understood what the Buddha meant after seeing the miracle of [a] single flower being life changing," writes Sue Patton Thoele in *The Mindful Woman.*

> My husband Gene and I had a trans-Pacific-ocean courtship. To help bridge the miles, he once sent me red roses. After my sons were asleep, I took the time to luxuriate in every aspect of the fullest rose, exploring its textures, colors, and the varying shapes of petals, stem, and stamen. To my surprise, tears of joy began to slip from my eyes, and I felt enveloped in love and connected to both the man who sent the roses and their creator as well... Thirty-some years later, I clearly

remember that particular rose and can revisit the profound sense of wonder and awe I experienced while focusing on it.

An interesting aspect of Thoele's story is that she is validating researchers' findings. Remembering one's original awe experience can bring back that feeling again, even years later.

Tiptoe Through the Tulips

Two years ago, I celebrated my milestone eightieth birthday by taking a river cruise in Europe. We arrived in Amsterdam a few days early specifically to see the tulips. We could not have timed our arrival any better. The April spring weather meant that the tulips at Keukenhof Gardens were at their peak.

At every turn, I was awed by the intricate patterns formed by these tall-standing beauties. Even professionally taken photos don't do justice to seeing them in person. The river cruise was wonderful, but nothing compared to the tulip excursion that produced one awe moment after another and a memory that will last a lifetime.

OPEN THE DOOR TO AWE

When you look at something closer, what do you see that perhaps you haven't seen before?

How has a closer look changed your perception of that object?

Recall one thing that you have come to know better as a result of paying close attention to it.

TAKE A HIKE

If you cannot find terrain magnificent enough to take your breath away, gravitate to a place that can at least increase your heartbeat.

—Gary Nabhan, *Songbirds, Truffles and Wolves*

As documented by research, Mother Nature is one of the best suppliers of awe. Therefore, getting close to nature can be one of the best ways to up your awe quotient. And it need not be hiking the Camino. Simply taking a walk in your local park, backyard garden, or even in a city street can be grand.

And if you can't get out, watch a nature video. That, according to researchers, has similar benefits to actually being in natural surroundings.

OPEN THE DOOR TO AWE

On Quora, contributor B. Barker posted some ideas of where to take an awe-inspiring walk:

Nature settings: Hike up a mountain with panoramic views. Walk along a trail lined with tall trees. Walk along the shore of an ocean, lake, river, or waterfall. Walk outside on a clear night and look up at the stars. Walk to a place where you can watch a sunset or sunrise.

Urban settings: Climb to the top of a skyscraper or look up in an area dense with tall buildings. Visit a historic monument. Explore a part of the city that you've never seen before. Tour a large ballpark or stadium. Go on a city art walk and explore different galleries. Visit the botanical gardens or a zoo to see plants and animal species you've never seen before. Walk around with no destination in mind and see where it takes you.

Indoor settings: Walk slowly around a museum, giving your full attention to each piece. Visit a planetarium or aquarium. Take a tour of a historic mansion, cathedral, or opera house.

STOP.
LOOK.
LISTEN.

LEND AN EAR

Spiritual teaching has always pointed to the fact that everything in creation has a sound, its own unique vibration. As conscious listeners we may perceive more and more of what the universe is saying to us by the simple act of listening. We can learn to appreciate each and every sound.

—Katharine Le Mee, *Chant*

When I was a year old, I had a mastoid operation on my right ear. There was no penicillin at the time otherwise the surgery would not be needed. For most of my life, I was told that I had no hearing in that ear.

Maybe it is the new technology that detected an ability to hear on that side. Whatever the reason, it was suggested that, in addition to having a hearing aid in my left ear, I get a one for the right ear too.

I was looking forward to fully hearing sounds that perhaps I've been missing for years. When I put on the second hearing aid, however, the noise was overwhelming. I had to run out of the kitchen when the table was being set or the dishwasher was being emptied. The noise of the dishes and the silverware was too much.

Although the sounds around us can be useful there are times when they become too much, especially when they drown out so much else in our life. It is then that we need to seek out silence.

I know this when I'm writing. I don't need to hear the garbage truck on the street, the traffic outside, or people chatting beneath my window. I just want to be with my thoughts, the words to cement those thoughts, and my computer to write them down. Thus, I frequently take out my hearing aids and put in earplugs.

Seeking awe is not much different from seeking the right words. Perhaps it is why we often find it during quieter times when we are walking in the woods, gently rocking in a hammock, or enthralled with a painting in a museum.

Quite Mind

None of us is going to have a quiet mind all the time. Nor should we even expect that of ourselves. However, we can choose minutes in which to be quietly and consciously mindful of experiences, people, ideas, and loveliness that bring a sense of awe and reverence to our hearts. Seeing the immeasurable beauty and wonder in our own neighborhoods can be awesome in its own right. We don't have to go to Hawaii to have our awe-o-meters rocket off the charts.

—**Sue Patton Thoele,** *The Mindful Woman*

Traffic Sounds

Many of us get bent out of shape in traffic jams. Probably because we have lost control; we have given up our power to the conditions of the road. Where we were once able to speed along at sixty-five miles an hour we are now at five miles an hour, or worse, at a standstill.

Perhaps we can't do much about the physicality of the situation, but we can alter it with our attitude, or as author Frederick Buechner describes in *The Clown in the Belfry*, allow it to take our breath away:

> It was gorgeous traffic; it was beautiful traffic—that's what was not usual. It was a beauty to see, to hear, to smell, even to be part of. It was so dazzlingly alive it all but took my breath away. It rattled and honked and chattered with life—the people, the colors of their clothes, the marvelous hodgepodge of their faces, all of it; the taxis, the shops, the blinding sidewalks. This spring day made everybody a celebrity—[Black, white, and Hispanic people], every last one of them. It made even the litter and clamor and turmoil of it a kind of miracle.

Symphony in the Meadow

"After a long, cold night and no breakfast," writes Sam Keen in his book *Sighting*,

> we heard a male bird advertise his virility by the intensity and vigor of his song. Different species of birds and insects roused themselves from sleep at different intervals and began warming up their vocal cords. At first, a few of the featured soloists and supporting vocalists began rehearsing: a host of Song Sparrows practiced the soprano melody; Purple Finches and lesser sparrows added chirps, tweets, and twitters; Mourning Doves crooned the antiphonal moan; ubiquitous crows provided the caws and cackles; and

woodpeckers delivered the percussion. As the morning began to warm up, insects beyond number furnished a rich drone composed of hums, buzzes, and the swish of wings. All of this was accompanied by the sighing of the wind and the gurgling of the brook. A few minutes after full dawn arrived, the cacophony seemed to end, and the thousand individual creatures began to tune their instruments to a single complex pattern. Gradually, an invisible conductor forged the discord into a unified composition—Symphony in the Meadow on Sugarloaf Mountain—that lasted until the sun was high and hot.

Keen asks us to contemplate, when did we abandon these rich sounds that called to us so easily in childhood?—"the quack, chirp, whinny, bark, whine, bleat, mew, cackle, hoot, honk, and warble of birds, the whisper or howl of the winds, the splash and swoosh of falling water?"

The Sound of Grains

In 1873, clergyman Francis Kilvert noted in his diary that crops have different "voices," depending on the time of day. He wrote, "As I walked along the field path I stopped to listen to the rustle and solemn whisper of the wheat, so different in its voice by day. The corn seemed to be praising God and whispering its evening prayer."

OPEN THE DOOR TO AWE

Listen to music. Any kind that moves you—from symphonies of the great composers to rap songs about making a difference in the world.

When in traffic, can you turn the cacophony of traffic noise into your personal symphony?

Next time it snows, see if you can hear the snowflakes falling?

AWE CATCHERS

A good way to restore wonder's voice is to select some common mute marvel like the electric light and do without it. Fumble and stumble around in the dark, then when properly prepared, flick the switch. Hear the soundless thunder of awe when pitch-black midnight suddenly becomes bright as high noon. Wow! While not as earth-shattering as a thunderclap, it is an earthbound rumble of wonder.

—Edward Hays, *A Book of Wonders*

Native American cultures hang a dream catcher over baby's cradles as protection. It is used to catch bad dreams before they reach the child. I found this charming story in Hugh Prather's *The Little Book of Letting Go*, about how a dream catcher helped a four-year-old who was having an unusual number of nightmares. Her father, who is not of Native American descent, gave one to her.

> A dream catcher is not always supposed to be hung above the dreamer but also in a spot where rays of sunlight will shine on it. The light melts away the trapped bad dreams like fog vanishing before the warmth of the morning sun. Our friend [the father] didn't see such a place, but he knew from Sarah's tone that this was an emergency. So, he hung it from the ceiling fan—which was neither directly above her nor in line with the light from the window.

> When I talked to him several months later, the dream catcher was still on the fan, and Sarah had not had a single nightmare.

If you are experiencing an unusual number of "day-mares," you might want to acquire an "awe-catcher," something that replaces your despair with delight. Your awe-catcher need not be elaborate or even sizable. But it must be personal. Something that will immediately change what you have been experiencing, like the dream catcher did for Sarah, and take you out of your distress. It could be as simple as a photo of your first grandchild or a time you successfully climbed to the top of Half Dome, or the autographed photo of your favorite entertainer.

TURN AWE ON

In her book *The Five Principles*, author Ellen Debenport, writes that "when we are focused on a particular outcome, it shows up... Not because the cheerful are rewarded by a supreme being. Not because magical thinking comes true. But because we live in a universe where our thoughts— conscious or unconscious—bring about the events of our lives."

For me, that makes perfect sense. After all, we are all energy. We tap into the energy of each other and we tap into the energy of the world.

Have you ever met someone you have never encountered before and somehow felt you have known them for years? Your energy, your vibrations are matching up. The same thing happens in the world. The energy you are putting out in the world matches up to what is already out there.

We often label that as a coincidence and something we can't scientifically explain, but like coincidences, chance meetings, or strokes of luck, they are merely energies matching up with each other.

Think of a light switch. When you turn it on, the light goes on. When you turn it off, the light goes off. Yet, even in the off position, there is electricity just behind the scenes waiting for you to turn on the switch to get its benefits. Awe is no different. It is there all the time waiting for you to acknowledge it.

OPEN THE DOOR TO AWE

Take an awecation: Psychologist Andy Tix suggests that families take "awecations" instead of just vacations. Travel, he notes, to places that might inspire awe. He says that "travel provides endless opportunities for awe because we are exposed to stimuli that are out of our typical routine." And "If you can't get away, look for local spots to explore."

Record your awe:

- Keep a journal of any experiences that take your breath away.

- Draw your awe: Paint or collage a picture of something that amazed you.

Share your awe: Tell others about the things or the people that have impacted your life.

Make an awe reminder card: Write a big letter "A" on a three-by-five-inch card. Put it in your pocket or purse. Whenever you come across it, let it be a reminder to look around for something awesome.

WHAT IS AWE, AFTER ALL?

The sense of wonder. That is our sixth sense.

—D. H. Lawrence, author

After exploring the many interpretations of the word *awe*, I returned to my literary agent's question about what awe means. What I found was that there really is no definitive answer. Yes, there are the dictionary definitions I provided at the opening of this book, but that seemed limiting to me.

The reason for that is because awe is often in the eye of the beholder. It can be a knock-your-socks moment for one person but not as jaw-dropping for another. It can be obvious to someone yet overlooked by someone else. It can be memorable, even life changing, or it can be fleeting and forgetful.

There are many moments in our life that can be awesome to us, like the birth of our child, but which may not be awesome to others. Someone who works in the maternity ward, for example, and sees numerous babies being born on a regular basis, may no longer experience the awe factor in the birthing process.

I suspect that age and interests can both have something to do with what is a potential awe moment and what is not. A female teenager, for example, might use the word *awesome* to describe meeting a popular young male singer, or group, in the music world. For a young male teenager, getting the autograph of a famous sports star might produce an awe rush. On the other hand, these encounters might not mean much to a senior who is not familiar with either the music or sports scene.

Another reason it is hard to come up with a conclusive meaning may be because the feeling of awe is often fleeting. In addition, when describing an awe moment, it can be hard to convey exactly what happened. They are frequently beyond words—so overwhelming that they are often indescribable. As one person I interviewed said, "How do you define awe when it's beyond the point of putting it into words?"

After researching awe for many months and asking many people about their awe experiences, the best conclusion I can make is two-fold:

- ✷ Awe is difficult to define.
- ✷ Awe is many things to many people.

That said, if I were pressed to answer what awe is, I would preface it by saying that since it is often associated with something big, grand, or unexplainable, and often expressed with an "Oh, my God" response, awe is (drumroll, please): "The presence of the Divine in the world."

FINAL WORDS OF AWE

The knowledgeable person lives with a question mark, and the man of awe and wonder lives with an exclamation mark.

—Osho, spiritual teacher

P.S.: Got to go now. It's time to do some awe-robics.

DEAR READER

Thank you so much for reading my book. I am honored that out of the thousands of books published each year, you have chosen to spend some time with this one.

As in all my writing, my goal is to help you have a richer and more enjoyable life. If you get just one thing from this book that helps you do that, then all the many hours I spent putting this book together will have been worth it.

Writing is a lonely business. Authors spend months, sometimes years, completing a book. Then, if they are lucky, their work gets published. The book is birthed into the world and they never know how it may have influenced a reader. It would therefore be thrilling to hear your response after reading *The Awe Factor*. My email address is: allen@allenklein.com.

I would also love to have you post a review on Amazon at tinyurl.com/y88nyq5p.

Thank you,
Allen

P.S. To show my appreciation for your support of my work, I'd like to send you an article I wrote titled "Three Questions You Need to Ask Yourself If You Want More Joy in Your Life." Simply email me at: allen@allenklein.com.

ABOUT THE AUTHOR

Allen Klein is an award-winning professional keynote speaker and bestselling author. He is a recipient of a Lifetime Achievement Award from the Association for Applied and Therapeutic Humor, a Certified Speaking Professional designation from the National Speakers Association, a Communication and Leadership Award from Toastmasters International, and is an inductee in the Hunter Hall of Fame at Hunter College, New York City.

Klein is also the author of thirty-one books including *The Healing Power of Humor, Change Your Life!: A Little Book of Big Ideas, You Can't Ruin My Day, Embracing Life After Loss, Positive Thoughts for Troubling Times*, and *The Joy of Simplicity*. In addition, he is a TEDx presenter on the power of intention. Klein's TEDx talk is available online: www.youtube.com/watch?v=rqPu52vWpJA&t=7s.

For more information about Klein's books or presentations, go to AllenKlein.com or contact him at allen@allenklein.com.

Mango Publishing, established in 2014, publishes an eclectic list of books by diverse authors—both new and established voices—on topics ranging from business, personal growth, women's empowerment, LGBTQ studies, health, and spirituality to history, popular culture, time management, decluttering, lifestyle, mental wellness, aging, and sustainable living. We were recently named 2019 *and* 2020's #1 fastest growing independent publisher by *Publishers Weekly.* Our success is driven by our main goal, which is to publish high quality books that will entertain readers as well as make a positive difference in their lives.

Our readers are our most important resource; we value your input, suggestions, and ideas. We'd love to hear from you—after all, we are publishing books for you!

Please stay in touch with us and follow us at:

Facebook: Mango Publishing

Twitter: @MangoPublishing

Instagram: @MangoPublishing

LinkedIn: Mango Publishing

Pinterest: Mango Publishing

Sign up for our newsletter at www.mangopublishinggroup. com and receive a free book!

Join us on Mango's journey to reinvent publishing, one book at a time.